500

italian dishes

500

italian dishes

the only compendium of italian dishes you'll ever need

Valentina Sforza

SELLERS
PUBLISHING

A Quintet Book

Published by Sellers Publishing, Inc.
161 John Roberts Road, South Portland, Maine 04106
For ordering information:
(800) 625-3386 Toll Free
(207) 772-6814 Fax
Visit our Web site: www.sellerspublishing.com
E-mail: rsp@rsvp.com

ISBN: 978-1-4162-0574-6
Library of Congress Control Number: 2010921818
QTT.THIT

This book was conceived, designed, and produced by
Quintet Publishing Limited
6 Blundell Street
London N7 9BH
United Kingdom

Food Stylist: Valentina Sforza
Photographer: Ian Garlick
Designer: Rod Teasdale
Art Director: Michael Charles
Editorial Assistants: Carly Beckerman, Holly Willsher
Managing Editor: Donna Gregory
Publisher: James Tavendale

10 9 8 7 6 5 4 3 2 1

Printed in China by 1010 Printing International Ltd.

contents

introduction

Italian food is such a favorite with people of all ages and backgrounds because, ultimately, it is food that comes straight from the heart. Italians are an emotional race, and nothing quite stirs up their feelings of love and passion as talking about their favorite dish or recent eating experience. Of course, there is really no such thing as Italian food per se, because Italy still holds on fiercely to all the regional differences of cooking styles, gastronomic traditions, and local ingredients that vary from one region to another, but the entire nation shares the same values when it comes to good, healthy food, cooked simply, but with love and pride.

To understand Italy's regional differences, you have to go back in history a little. The unification of Italy took place in the 1860s. Before this, the country was a confusing collection of states, dukedoms, and principalities, with many bloody battles and ever-changing boundary lines. After the unification, 20 separate regions were created. For me, the ingredients and the cooking methods of each region reflect certain aspects of the local history. It is this, plus the geography and climate, that gives each region of Italy its very own culinary identity, and thus gives us not just one but 20 different cuisines to choose from.

One of the many things about cooking Italian food that never fails to thrill me is how the cooking always reflects, respects, and understands the seasons of the year and the precious gifts that are available season by season. Acknowledging and embracing each of the seasons and their produce means that you can cook with anticipation. My earliest memories of the huge meals prepared at home in Tuscany are the discussions about what was in season and what wasn't. Whatever was in season was considered fit for the table, while anything out of season was simply postponed. The first *nespole* (loquats) of the spring were something to get excited about after months and months of citrus fruit, and they were heralded by the last oranges of the winter – the dark purple, almost black *tarocchi* (blood oranges). The long, jade

green, frosted cardoons of early winter days were considered truly special; mushrooms and game were eagerly anticipated and received in the fall; and all the glowing fruits of the summer were as much a part of the season as the lopsided deckchairs in the vine-clad garden, the irritating mosquitoes, and the long beach days punctuated with ice cream.

As a cooking teacher, I can tell you honestly that cooking classes, at whatever level, can teach you about technique, can introduce you to ingredients you might not have previously considered, and can take you through the most daunting of recipes. The one thing that cannot be taught is how to cook instinctively, like an Italian. A real cook, a cook who is genuinely outstanding, is a cook who uses his or her heart and intuition in the kitchen. This is how Italians cook. It is the only way in which they know how to cook, because they live to eat! Their enjoyment of food and of cooking is seasoned with true passion, flair, and joy that go far beyond the necessity to merely keep body and soul together and stave off hunger.

I am a "don't mess with it" kind of cook, the sort who, like all the Italian cooks I know and respect, simply chooses the best possible ingredients that are available at the time, and then does as little as possible to them. I am proud of this, because in this way, the ingredients are allowed to sing out and give of their absolute best. In this book, I've brought together a collection of recipes that are among those I consider to be the very best recipes that Italy has to offer. They are almost all quick and easy to prepare so that you can have a busy lifestyle and still eat delicious food. This is, after all, the way most Italians eat.

I hope that you'll enjoy all the recipes contained in this collection. I wish you countless happy meals around the table with your loved ones, and many hours of joy in the kitchen discovering and exploring these recipes, and elaborating upon them as much as you wish, in order that they may become as much a part of your favorite repertoire as they are of mine.

eating italian-style

In the case of a traditional Italian meal, containing many courses, first to be served would always be an antipasto. This would be a small dish, just enough to get the taste buds titillated. Following this would come the primo, which is usually pasta or risotto, but could also be gnocchi or a soup. After this would come the secondo, which can be meat (i.e., meat, poultry, or game), fish (or seafood), or a complex and substantial vegetable and/or cheese dish. Following this there could be a platter of cheeses, or even just one cheese, often with fresh fruit such as pears and/or nuts, and finally the dolce, or dessert.

This gargantuan feast is not the sort of meal that most Italians would or could nowadays settle down to eat on an everyday basis, but it is the sort of meal one should expect to be served for a special occasion such as a wedding reception, a first communion, or a special birthday or anniversary. Often, this sort of meal is served at lunchtime, which means that an afternoon siesta would be almost statutory, and at the end of the meal various digestive liqueurs and the ubiquitous tiny cup of espresso coffee would always be offered.

The chapters in this book are therefore arranged in such a way that makes it easy to structure a balanced menu for an entire traditional Italian meal simply by selecting favorite recipes from each chapter. On the other hand, you could also create a much shorter menu by choosing just two or three recipes from throughout the book, or indeed just choose one recipe at a time. Buon appetito!

equipment

pasta pots & pasta machines

To cook pasta, it's not necessary to have a "pasta pot" with a removable strainer. You simply need a really big pot so your pasta can move freely while it cooks. It must have a lid to help bring the water quickly back to a boil once the pasta has been added.

I would recommend a hand-turned pasta machine rather than an electric, as the results are always better. I also stress the importance of buying one that is made in Italy and of a reputable brand such as Imperia. Never wash your pasta machine, or it will rust internally and seize up forever. To keep it clean, brush the flour off carefully with a clean paintbrush, wipe with a clean dry cloth, and return to a dry cupboard, preferably in its box, until the next time you need it.

skillets & saucepans

It is good to have a selection of different-sized saucepans and skillets for the recipes in this book. Stainless steel is best, but enamel-lined is also good. Make sure you have at least one good-quality nonstick skillet in your collection.

mixing bowls, colanders & sieves

Having a wide variety of different sizes of mixing bowls is always useful. They can be used for holding ingredients until required, or for mixing ingredients together. A big colander is always more useful than a small one, especially when draining pasta. It is also a good idea to have two sieves, one that is very fine for dry ingredients, and one with larger holes, preferably a chinois (a triangular-shaped sieve with a point) for straining stocks or sauces.

knives & cutting boards

The most important item to have in your kitchen is a good set of knives. You will need a big chef's knife (9-inch minimum length) for chopping comfortably and accurately and also for slicing thinly, and a small cook's knife (4- to 6-inch minimum length), which can be the same shape as the larger knife and can be used for paring, peeling, and slicing. You will also need a small knife with a serrated blade for cutting tomatoes. Finally, as far as knives are concerned, a good bread knife and a spatula are essential.

You can't cut directly on your counter, so you'll need cutting boards. Raw meat, fish, and poultry need to be trimmed and cut on a separate board from vegetables, fruit, cheese, and bread, so at least two boards are really essential.

measuring cups, spoons & scales

Although most Italians are quite disarmingly easygoing about quantities, happy to add a pinch of this and a handful of that with ease and flair, it may be better, at least initially, to measure ingredients with some degree of accuracy. So it is useful to have a set of measuring spoons for small quantities, measuring cups for liquids, a set of solids measuring cups, and a pair of scales.

other equipment

A good sharp grater is always important for both grating and zesting citrus fruits and cheese, and a small hand juicer is also very useful. A good pair of sharp scissors is vital for performing a wide variety of tasks. Add to this list a couple of pairs of tongs, including ones with comblike teeth for spaghetti; a ladle; some heatproof rubber spatulas; balloon whisks; pastry brushes and heatproof brushes; and various spoons—slotted, large metal, and wooden.

Items specifically for cooking Italian food are the rocking chopper with two handles known in Italian as *la mezzaluna* (literally translated, "half-moon"); a pasta claw for stirring, separating, and ultimately serving pasta efficiently; a food mill, known in Italian as *passatutto* and often referred to in English as a mouli, which is used for passing sauces or other ingredients; and a mortar and pestle for grinding.

As far as electrical items are concerned, a stick or immersion blender is always very useful, as is an electric handheld whisk.

basic ingredients

flour & pasta

The type of flour that you will find in Italy for everyday cooking will be "00," literally double zero and indicating that it contains absolutely no flour bran, and is therefore pure white. It is also sometimes called *fior di farina*. Then there is "0" flour, which is less pure white because it still contains a small percentage of bran and is therefore heavier, and grittier in texture. It can be used for bread-making. *Farina di semola* is flour made from hard (durum) wheat that is used specifically for pasta-making. Do not confuse it with semolina, which is made with normal soft grain wheat that has not been milled to the point of flour.

All these kinds of flours are available outside of Italy, but plain white all-purpose flour makes a perfectly good substitute for Italian 00 flour. Still, different flours have surprisingly different properties, so always use your judgment when working with a recipe, and adjust ratios of flour to liquids and fats to flour to get the consistency called for in the recipe. Generally speaking, whole wheat and whole-grain flour are not used very much in traditional Italian cooking.

The main difference between dried pasta and fresh pasta is that the former is made with durum wheat flour and water and has to be made in factory conditions in order to achieve the right results. Fresh pasta contains eggs, and can be made entirely out of soft wheat flour or a combination of the two types of flour (durum wheat flour and soft wheat flour). There are more than 650 different shapes of pasta available, yet the most popular remains the humble spaghetti!

rice & polenta

To make the great Italian rice dish called risotto, it is important to have the right kind of rice. A risotto made with the wrong kind of rice will not have the right level of creaminess. It is the starch falling from the grains as the rice cooks, blending with the stock, wine, and other flavors, that gives the risotto its velvety texture. It is never necessary to add cream to a risotto.

Polenta is flour made from milling a special kind of maize. It comes in either white or yellow varieties and in three different degrees of texture — fine, medium, and coarse. The choice between all of these largely comes down to personal preference and availability. You can, of course, buy quick-cook polenta, which takes much less time to cook, and also precooked polenta that can be sliced and grilled or fried as required.

eggs

The only special kind of eggs sold in Italy, and in some good Italian delicatessens elsewhere in the world, are those with an especially bright orange yolk that are sold specifically for making fresh pasta, as they give the dough that marvelous golden yellow color. It is not, however, necessary to have these eggs for making pasta, because it can be made perfectly well with any kind of eggs, though the end result may be a bit paler.

All eggs in these recipes are extra-large size.

oil & butter

Olive oil is vital for giving Italian food its unique Italian flavor. Extra-virgin olive oil contains the lowest level of oleic acid and is considered to be the best. Olive oil is much less intensely flavored and may have water added to it, which makes it thinner in texture. Use sunflower seed or other seed oil for deep-frying. As far as butter is concerned, you should always use butter for cooking, as the salt will reach the burning point before the fat contained in the butter.

cheese

Parmesan cheese (which, for Italians, is either *parmigiano reggiano* or *grana padano*) is essential for the recipes contained in this book. Parmesan is a very hard, grainy, dry cheese that is used finely grated or shaved in many recipes, but is also delicious eaten on its own as part of a cheese board.

Another essential cheese for Italian cooking is mozzarella, a stretched-curd cheese that is white and springy and can be used either raw or in cooking. Made with either cow's or buffalo milk (*mozzarella di bufala*), it needs to be kept fresh in milk or water or whey. It can also be dried and aged for cooking, when it is called scamorza.

Other essential Italian cheeses you will need for these recipes (and I do recommend you use the authentic Italian-made versions of all these cheeses) are: Pecorino, which is similar to Parmesan but made with ewe's milk cheese; mascarpone, a very thick, sweet, and creamy cheese; ricotta, a slightly granular, sweetish, soft cheese; Gorgonzola, a blue, soft, runny cheese available in a sweet (dolce) version and a more piquant version (piccante); fontina, a medium-soft cheese with a lovely buttery flavor from Val d'Aosta; and Emmenthal or groviera, which are both nutty, medium-hard cheeses that melt deliciously in the cooking process.

fruits, vegetables, herbs & spices

All fruit, vegetables, and herbs should be seasonal and sourced locally whenever possible. Essential ingredients for any Italian are onions, celery, carrots, garlic, and, of course, tomatoes. Besides fresh tomatoes, canned are widely used when really good tomatoes are not in season. Canned tomatoes come whole or chopped. In the case of whole canned tomatoes, I always recommend you open the can, tip the tomatoes into a bowl, and check through them before adding them to your recipe. Removing and discarding unripe sections of tomato, odd pieces of skin, hard calyxes, or even overlooked pieces of stalk before adding the tomatoes will hugely improve the end result. This is obviously impossible with chopped canned tomatoes. Tomato paste consists of a concentrated tomato purée, which lends intensity of flavor and sweetness.

Also essential are fresh herbs—especially flat-leaf parsley, basil, sage, and rosemary. Oregano is always used as a dried herb in Italy, because drying it brings out its uniquely sour, sharp flavor. The spices you will need are nutmeg, dried chile pepper, freshly ground black pepper, and cinnamon.

meat, poultry & seafood

In terms of fresh meat, poultry, and game, try to make sure the meat you buy is of good quality and from a traceable source, preferably organic but certainly chemical-free. It is always better to buy from a butcher, as he or she will not only be able to guide and advise you around the various cuts available, but will also be able to carry out more tricky tasks such as boning or trimming for you.

Cured meats, such as pancetta, guanciale, bresaola, Parma ham, various kinds of salami, mortadella, and raw Italian sausages like luganega are really essential for many Italian dishes, and most of them offer a simple way of preparing an antipasto. Prosciutto crudo is the generic term for cured, air-dried ham, of which the one from Parma is considered to be the best. Pancetta and guanciale are two different kinds of Italian bacon, and are interchangeable. Bresaola is one of the few Italian cured meats that is not made out of pork; instead, it is made using beef.

For seafood, it is generally best to use a fishmonger for your needs as it is more likely that there will be a wider choice and that much of the fish will be from traceable sources. They will always be happy to guide and advise, and will do jobs like gutting, scaling, and filleting for you as required.

wine

Many of the dishes in this book use wine as a flavoring ingredient and sometimes also as a liquid for cooking. Mostly, the wines used are dry red and white wine, but there is also the semisweet Sicilian wine called Marsala, from the port of the same name. If this is hard to find, the best alternative is to use Madeira or a semisweet sherry. In some other recipes vermouth is an ingredient, by which I mean something like Martini or Cinzano, red or white, sweet or dry.

making fresh pasta

You will need, per person, 1 extra-large egg and 1/4 lb. all-purpose flour — but bear in mind that no two batches of flour are identical, and that no two eggs are ever quite the same either, so you may end up having to add more egg or more flour to your mixture.

To make pasta dough, put flour in a pile on a work surface and plunge your fist into the center to make a hollow. Break eggs into a bowl and whisk together, then pour them into the hollow in the flour. Using your fingers, begin to knead eggs roughly into flour. Then use your hands to knead everything together.

This is not like making pastry, so this is not the moment for a delicate approach. On the other hand, if you are too heavy-handed, you will cause the dough to dry out too much and it will never roll out smoothly. Knead with a steady, medium pressure until you have a really smooth, pliable ball of dough. Then, let rest under a clean cloth for about 20 minutes to relax the gluten and make the dough more manageable.

After resting the dough, roll it out as thinly as possible with a heavy, long rolling pin. Continue to roll the dough over and over again until it is really elastic, smooth, and shiny. It should cool down considerably as you work it (you will feel it dropping in temperature as you go). When it is ready, the sheet of dough will feel like a brand new, wrung-out, damp chamois leather, but it must not be brittle. Keep it moist by covering it with a slightly damp clean cloth when you are not working with it.

If you use a hand-cranked pasta machine instead of a rolling pin, knead eggs and flour together into a rough-textured ball of dough. Rest the dough for 20 minutes, then cover with a very slightly damp cloth after breaking off a piece about the size of a small fist. Flatten this piece with your hands and push it through the widest setting on the pasta machine. Fold in half and repeat. Do this three times. Move the machine down to the next setting. Repeat three times. Continue in this way, changing the setting after every three times, until you hear the pasta snap as it is going between the rollers. At this point you can forget about folding it in half each time, as the surface tension is now correct.

Continue to wind it through the rollers to the last setting on the machine, depending on how fine you want it to be. Lay the sheet of pasta carefully on a floured surface. If you are not filling the pasta, it needs to be left to dry, uncovered, until it feels papery before being cut into the desired shape, otherwise it will be impossible to stop all the strands sticking together. If, on the other hand, you are going to fill the pasta, do so immediately, while it is still moist enough to stick together. Now take another small lump of dough and begin again.

To freeze fresh pasta: Open-freeze on trays, then bag it up and label. Keeps for about 1 month once frozen.

stock

Good stocks are at the foundation of good cooking, especially when it comes to sauces, risotto, soups, and stews. Making beef, chicken, or vegetable stock is not difficult; here are basic recipes. An Italian Bouquet Garni is a simple package of bay leaf, sprigs of sage, rosemary, and thyme all tied together with plain string, or wrapped in cheesecloth.

beef or veal stock

3 1/4 lbs. beef or veal bones
1 onion, quartered
2 carrots, quartered
1 leek, quartered
2 celery stalks, quartered

1 tomato, quartered
1 bouquet garni
6 peppercorns
1 pinch salt
5 pints cold water

Place all the ingredients in a large pot. Bring to a boil, then let simmer, skimming off any scum that forms on the surface. Simmer for about 4 hours. Then pour through a sieve into a bowl, pressing down on the pieces in the sieve to extract every bit of flavor. Cool, then skim off any congealed fat. Can be refrigerated for up to 3 days or frozen for 6 months. For a richer, brown stock, roast bones first in a 450°F oven for about 45 minutes. Add vegetables to bones about halfway through. Baste with a little water if necessary, then transfer to a stockpot, add the remaining water, and continue as above.
Makes about 5 pints

chicken stock

about 1 1/2 lbs. cooked (e.g., carcass from roast
    chicken) or raw chicken
1 onion, quartered, or 1 leek, halved lengthwise
2 stalks celery, halved
2 carrots, halved

few sprigs fresh parsley
6 peppercorns
3 pints cold water
2 pinches salt

Put all ingredients in a stockpot. Bring to a boil, then cover and simmer for about 2 hours.
Skim the surface often to remove any scum. Remove from heat and cool completely, then
strain into a bowl, pressing down on pieces in the sieve to extract every last bit of flavor.
Once cooled, it will be easy to remove fat from the surface, as it will have solidified. Can
be refrigerated for up to 3 days or frozen for about 6 months.
Makes about 3 pints

vegetable stock

2 carrots, quartered
1 large onion, halved
2 stalks celery, quartered
2 tomatoes, halved
2 or 3 cabbage leaves, quartered

1/2 leek, trimmed, left whole
8 lettuce leaves, halved
2 pinches salt
2 pints cold water

You can use any vegetables you like in a vegetable stock; it is a good way to use up raw
vegetables that are a bit tired or left over. Use the list above simply as suggestions.
Clean and wash all vegetables, then place them in a stockpot with salt and water. Bring to
a boil slowly, then simmer, covered, for about 1 1/2 hours. Remove from the heat and cool
completely, then strain into a bowl. Press down on the solids in the sieve to extract every last
bit of flavor. Can be refrigerated for up to 3 days or frozen for about 6 months.
Makes about 2 pints

antipasti e insalate
antipasti & salads

Traditionally, Italian meals begin with a light antipasto before the first course, the primo — usually pasta or risotto — which for most Italians is the most important part of the meal. Antipasti are something to enjoy while the primo finishes cooking in the kitchen.

pane con la farina di polenta
bread with polenta flour

see variations page 64

Putting polenta into bread dough with wheat flour to make polenta bread means that the bread will take on a slightly grainier texture, have a lovely golden yellow appearance, and will also last longer before becoming stale.

2 1/2 oz. fresh yeast
1 cup warm water
pinch granulated sugar
2 1/4 cups all-purpose flour

1 1/4 cups polenta
sea salt
2–3 tsp. olive oil

Mix yeast and water together, then add sugar and about 2 tablespoons of the all-purpose flour. Place the yeast mixture in a warm place for about 30 minutes to activate. Pour polenta and remaining flour onto a work surface. When the yeast mixture is fizzing gently and has formed something of a head, like on a glass of beer, knead it energetically into the polenta and flour on the working surface. Add more water as required to make a very soft dough. Add salt and oil and knead hard for about 10 minutes. Transfer the very soft, elastic, slightly shiny dough to a large floured bowl, cover with plastic wrap (oil the underside of the plastic lightly to prevent it sticking to the rising dough), and return it to warm place to rise again for about 2 hours or until doubled. Preheat oven to 375°F. Pull dough into two sections with well-oiled hands. Shape into rough rounds or whatever shape you like — long and narrow, braided, or oval. Stroke surface gently with a handful of olive oil and water mixed together. Bake on oiled and polenta-scattered baking sheets for about 15 minutes, or a little more or less time based on the size of the loaf. Tap the bottom of the bread and listen for a hollow ring to let you know it is cooked through. Cool on a wire rack to allow the steam to escape.

Makes 2 medium-sized loaves

focaccia
focaccia

see variations page 65

This deliciously oily, salty flat bread comes from the sunny region of Liguria on the Italian Riviera. Focaccia can be thick or thin, stuffed, topped, or plain – finished off with just oil and coarse salt.

4 1/4 cups white bread flour	pinch granulated sugar
2 1/2 oz. fresh yeast	2–3 tsp. olive oil
1 1/4 cups warm water	sea salt

Tip all the flour out on to the work surface. Mix yeast and water together, then add the sugar. When the yeast mixture is fizzing gently and has formed something of a head, like on a glass of beer, knead it energetically into flour. Add a little more water as required. Add salt and oil and knead hard for about 10 minutes. Transfer the soft, elastic, slightly shiny dough to a large floured bowl, cover with plastic wrap (oil the underside of the plastic lightly to prevent it sticking to the rising dough), and return it to warm place to rise again for about 2 hours or until doubled. Pull dough apart into sections with well-oiled hands and shape into rough rounds, flattening them between your palms. Lay them onto a well-oiled baking sheet, flattening them out as much as possible with your fingertips, bearing in mind they will rise again and become even thicker, and let rise again in warm place for another hour.

Preheat oven to 425°F. Force shallow dips in the surface of the focaccia with your fingertips, flattening and dimpling the surface as much as possible. Add oil and salt generously, and bake for about 10–12 minutes, or until the top is golden and crisp and the focaccia moves freely on the baking sheet. Slide off baking sheet to cool until required.

Makes 6 small, 3 medium, or 1 large focaccia

la panzanella
tuscan bread salad

see variations page 66

This lovely, light Tuscan salad makes fantastic use of what was once a most precious commodity — stale bread. In Tuscany, this is essential summer eating, as it is light and delicious while still being filling enough to stave off hunger pangs.

8 slices rustic white bread, stale
4 fist-sized ripe, fresh tomatoes
1 large onion
1 large cucumber

handful of basil leaves, washed and dried
extra-virgin olive oil, to taste
red wine vinegar, to taste
sea salt and freshly ground black pepper

Soak the bread in cold water for about 15 minutes. Squeeze the bread dry in a clean cloth. Slice tomatoes, onion, and cucumber. Tear the basil into small pieces. In a large bowl, mix the damp bread with the tomatoes, onion, cucumber, and basil. Dress with olive oil, vinegar, and salt and pepper to taste. Mix together very well and let the salad stand for about 30 minutes before serving.

Serves 6

insalata di asparagi e prosciutto di parma

asparagus & parma ham salad

see variations page 67

The marriage of asparagus with the sweet-yet-salty taste of Parma ham is like a match made in heaven. Keep the asparagus slightly crisp so you get a real contrast of textures as well as flavors. The cool blandness of the mozzarella serves as the perfect background.

1 large bunch fresh asparagus
4 large slices Parma ham
5 tbsp. extra-virgin olive oil

2 tbsp. good-quality, thick balsamic vinegar
sea salt and freshly ground black pepper
1 ball fresh buffalo mozzarella

You will need enough asparagus to end up with 2 large or 4 smaller stalks per person, or a combination of these. Peel very large asparagus with a vegetable peeler and trim, wash, and dry them all. Remove any woody sections of stalks. Cut the Parma ham into enough pieces to wrap each stalk.

Heat a griddle pan or light a grill or broiler to medium heat. Brush asparagus all over with olive oil and grill on all sides, turning frequently, until soft all the way through and very slightly blackened on the outside. Cool, then wrap each stalk in Parma ham, and arrange on a dish. Sprinkle with balsamic vinegar, olive oil, and salt and pepper to taste, then tear the mozzarella into pieces, scatter on top, and serve at once.

Serves 6

rotolini di bresaola con la rucola
cured beef rolls with arugula

see variations page 68

It is always best, if you can, to buy your bresaola (an air-cured beef) from a whole piece of meat, which is then sliced professionally in front of you. This will always taste better than buying bresaola in a neat plastic package. The secret with cured meats is to try to eat them as soon as possible after slicing. This recipe for bresaola–arugula rolls is a really lovely way to enjoy this delicious specialty from the Valtellina area of Lombardy, in Northern Italy. Don't be tempted to make it too far in advance, or the dressing on the arugula leaves will cause them to wilt and lose their crispness.

2 handfuls arugula leaves
3 oz. Parmesan, finely shaved
juice of 1/2 lemon, strained, or
    2 tsp. best-quality balsamic vinegar
extra-virgin olive oil to taste

freshly ground black pepper
7 oz. bresaola, thinly sliced
fresh chives
wedges of lemon, to serve

Gently mix together the arugula and Parmesan. Dress lightly with lemon juice or balsamic vinegar, olive oil, and pepper. Wrap up a small amount in the bresaola slices to make neat little rolls and tie each one closed with chives. Arrange the rolls on a platter and garnish with wedges of lemon to serve.

Serves 6

insalata di finocchio, salame e olive
fennel, salami & olive salad

see variations page 69

Salami is one of the most ancient elements in the wide gastronomic range of Italian products. It has very old traditions that have evolved over the centuries, with many distinct regional specialties, which can be identified by the way in which the meat has been minced — fine, medium, or coarse — and by the addition of other flavorings such as garlic, chile, fennel seeds, or wine. Generally speaking, salamis have a long, rounded sausage shape and come in many different sizes according to type.

2 fennel heads, cleaned and thinly sliced
large handful pitted black olives
12 slices chile-flavored salami, cut into strips
for the dressing
juice of 2 oranges
grated zest of 1 orange

1/2 tsp. prepared mustard (preferably
   Italian Savora)
sea salt and freshly ground black pepper
   to taste
1 cup extra-virgin olive oil

Toss fennel, olives, and salami strips together in a large serving bowl. Combine the dressing ingredients in a jar, screw on the top, and shake until all the ingredients have blended together. Pour over the salad and toss everything together thoroughly. Let stand for about 30 minutes before serving, to allow the flavors to develop.

Serves 6

insalata di riso
rice salad

see variations page 70

This rice salad is an absolute classic that appears on countless menus throughout the whole country. Especially popular in summertime, it is a lovely light way to start a meal.

1 cup long-grain rice
1 carrot
1 medium potato, peeled
1 small zucchini, topped and tailed
2 oz. fresh green beans (haricots vert), topped and tailed
2 hard-boiled eggs, finely chopped
4 anchovy fillets, rinsed, dried, and chopped

1 tbsp. capers, rinsed and coarsely chopped
2 tbsp. roughly chopped green or black olives
1 tbsp. chopped fresh flat-leaf parsley
for the dressing
6 tbsp. extra-virgin olive oil
2 tsp. lemon juice
sea salt and freshly ground black pepper

Boil the rice in lightly salted water for 18 minutes, or until tender. Cut carrot, potato, and zucchini into equal-size cubes and the beans into same-size pieces. Boil in a separate saucepan until tender. Drain the rice and all the vegetables thoroughly and separately.

Mix the warm, drained rice with the eggs, anchovies, capers, olives, parsley, and vegetables. Use a very large spoon to distribute everything evenly. Mix the olive oil and lemon juice together thoroughly, then pour over the salad. Toss well and season to taste with salt and pepper. Let stand for at least 1 hour before serving. If you need to chill the salad, bring it back to room temperature before serving.

Serves 6

insalata di tonno e fagioli
tuna & bean salad

see variations page 71

A classic starter, especially in Rome, this tuna and bean salad definitely benefits from being left to stand for a while to allow the flavors to really blend. Use tuna that is of the best possible quality.

10 oz. canned, fresh, or dried borlotti (or cranberry) beans
10 oz. canned tuna in olive oil, flaked
1 large red onion, thinly sliced

2 tbsp. chopped fresh flat-leaf parsley
5 tbsp. olive oil
1 tbsp. white or red wine vinegar
sea salt and freshly ground black pepper

If using canned beans, drain and rinse in cold water. If using fresh or dried borlotti beans, you need to soak them in cold fresh water. Dried beans need to be soaked overnight; fresh beans do not require as much soaking. Drain the beans, then cook them in fresh water for 5 minutes. Drain and rinse, then cook slowly in fresh water until tender. Do not salt the water until the beans are tender, or the skins will toughen.

Mix the cooled beans with the flaked tuna. Add the onion and parsley, and mix together. Dress with olive oil, vinegar, and salt and pepper. Mix together thoroughly. Let the salad stand for about 30 minutes, then serve with plenty of crusty bread to mop up the juices.

Serves 6

insalata di frutti di mare
seafood salad

see variations page 72

This classic seafood salad is good served just warm, or it can be made a few hours ahead and served cold. Vary the choice of seafood according to personal taste.

7 oz. fresh squid, cleaned and cut into neat
   strips and rings
2 lbs. fresh mussels, scrubbed and cleaned
1 lb. fresh baby clams, scrubbed and cleaned
6 oz. small fresh shrimp
4 large fresh shrimp

for the dressing
1 lemon, halved
6 tbsp. extra-virgin olive oil
3 tbsp. chopped fresh flat-leaf parsley
freshly ground black pepper
sea salt

Boil the squid in salted water for 25–30 minutes, or until tender. Drain and put in a large bowl. Steam the mussels and clams for about 8 minutes, discarding any that do not open. Wash the small shrimp well and cover with cold water in a saucepan. Bring to a boil and cook for 1 minute, then drain and cool before shelling. Add to the bowl with the squid. Remove the clams and mussels from their shells and put them in the bowl with the shrimp and squid. Toss together.

Boil the 4 large shrimp for 2 minutes, then drain, devein, and cool. Set aside.

Squeeze the juice from half the lemon and slice the other half to use as a garnish. Add the juice to the mixed seafood with the oil, parsley, and pepper to taste. Add salt only after mixing. Serve garnished with the 4 large shrimp and lemon slices.

Serves 6

insalata caprese
tricolor salad

see variations page 73

This absolutely classic salad originates on the beautiful island of Capri and is truly an unforgettable dish when made with the local richly flavored tomatoes, the soft and silky local buffalo mozzarella, and the intensely perfumed basil grown on the volcanic terrain. It is a lesson in the use of very few but perfect ingredients put together with simple skill.

2 very large or 4 medium-sized firm ripe
   tomatoes, washed well
4 balls fresh mozzarella or 3 balls buffalo
   mozzarella, drained

6 tbsp. extra-virgin olive oil
about 24 leaves fresh basil, torn into
   small pieces
sea salt and freshly ground black pepper

Slice the tomatoes and mozzarella into even-sized slices, cubes, or chunks. Put them into a salad bowl and toss together gently. Sprinkle with olive oil and mix together again. Add the basil, torn into pieces. Sprinkle with salt and pepper to taste and mix again. Let stand for about 15 minutes before serving. Alternatively, arrange the sliced tomatoes flat on a platter, cover each slice of tomato with a slice of mozzarella, and scatter basil over the slices before dressing with olive oil, sea salt, and freshly ground black pepper.

Serves 6

insalata di rucola, pere e parmigiano
arugula, pear & parmesan salad

see variations page 74

This pretty salad has a lovely combination of flavors. The sweetness of the pears really highlights the peppery quality of the arugula, and the saltiness of the Parmesan brings the whole thing together.

4 handfuls arugula leaves
2 small, firm pears, peeled and sliced
3 oz. Parmesan, thinly shaved

1 tbsp. balsamic vinegar
6 tbsp. olive oil
sea salt and freshly ground black pepper

Arrange the arugula leaves on each of 6 plates. Place the pear slices around and among the leaves. Scatter with Parmesan shavings. Sprinkle with balsamic vinegar. Mix the olive oil with salt and pepper until emulsified. Sprinkle over the salad and serve immediately.

Serves 6

insalata di pomodori e olive con crema di olive
tomato & olive salad with olive paste

see variations page 75

To make the olive pâté for this tomato and olive salad, just process a jar (about 8oz) of pitted black olives, drained, with a little lemon juice, a clove of peeled garlic, chopped fresh parsley, and salt and pepper until smooth.

6 large tomatoes, peeled and cut into chunks
2 small cucumbers, peeled and cut into same
   size as tomatoes
2 large red onions, diced very small
3–4 tbsp. coarsely chopped fresh flat-leaf
   parsley

6 tbsp. chopped black olives
for the dressing
2 tbsp. black olive pâté (recipe above)
2 tbsp. lemon juice
6 tbsp. extra-virgin olive oil
sea salt and freshly ground black pepper

Put the tomatoes, cucumbers, and onions into a large bowl and mix together gently. Add the parsley and combine with the vegetables. Add the olives and mix well.

To make the dressing, combine black olive pâté, lemon juice, and olive oil. If the mixture is too sticky, add a little more olive oil and mix thoroughly. Add salt and pepper to taste. Pour the dressing onto the vegetables and combine. The juices from the vegetables should help loosen the dressing as you mix it through the salad. Serve at once, with crusty bread.

Serves 6

carpaccio di zucchini
raw zucchini salad

see variations page 76

This delicious raw zucchini salad is perfect as a starter or served as a main course with a platter of cured meats. Make sure the slices are very thin and well coated with the other ingredients.

8 medium zucchini
sea salt
large handful fresh flat-leaf parsley,
    finely chopped

1/2 lb. Parmesan, freshly shaved
juice of 1/2 lemon
7 tbsp. extra-virgin olive oil
freshly ground black pepper

Slice the zucchini lengthwise into strips. Lay in a large colander, sprinkled with salt in several layers. Place a plate on top of the zucchini and a weight, such as a can of tomatoes, on top of the plate. Let drain for about 1 hour. Then rinse off the salt carefully, dry the slices thoroughly, and arrange on a large plate in slightly overlapping layers. Scatter with parsley and Parmesan. Sprinkle with lemon juice, olive oil, and salt and pepper to taste.

Serves 6

carciofi alla romana
baked artichokes

see variations page 77

This delicious way of serving artichokes is typical of the cooking style of the city of Rome, with plenty of strong, robust flavors like garlic, lemon, and mint to really bring the taste of the vegetable to life.

12 fist-sized fresh artichokes
2 lemons, quartered
sea salt and freshly ground black pepper
12 cloves garlic, thinly sliced
large handful fresh mint, washed and dried

zest of 1 lemon, finely chopped
about 6 cups water
about 6 tbsp. dry white wine
about 1/2 cup olive oil

Preheat oven to 500°F. Prepare the artichokes by removing all external hard leaves and removing the choke from the center. Rub them all over with the quartered lemons and set them upright in a wide baking dish. Place a few slices of garlic inside each artichoke. Strip the leaves off the mint and distribute the mint leaves and lemon peel among the artichokes. Sprinkle generously with salt and pepper. Pour the water, wine, and oil over them. Cover the dish with aluminum foil and bake for about 30–40 minutes or until almost soft all the way through. Turn the artichokes on their side to help them finish cooking, remove the aluminum foil and return to the oven for 10 minutes. Baste occasionally. Don't let them dry out, and keep adding water or white wine if necessary. Serve hot or cold.

Serves 6

arancini di riso
rice croquettes

see variations page 78

These delicious little balls of rice, named "little oranges" because of their shape and color, are very much a part of the Sicilian menu. They can be made in any size to suit all occasions.

about 2 1/4 cups cooled plain risotto
    (page 126, risotto alla parmigiana)
about 1/4 lb. cooked peas
3 oz. sautéed mushrooms
3 oz. chopped Parma ham
3 1/2 oz. diced mozzarella

3 tbsp. all-purpose flour
3 eggs, beaten
6 tbsp. fine, dry, white bread crumbs
vegetable, canola, or sunflower seed oil for
    deep-frying or olive oil for brushing prior
    to baking

Mix the cold risotto with the peas, mushrooms, and Parma ham. Roll the mixture into balls about the size of small oranges. Push a piece of mozzarella into the center of each ball, and make sure it is well covered. Roll into flour, then beaten eggs, then bread crumbs. Make sure the balls are firm and well-coated. Deep-fry in oil in a large skillet until golden and crisp all over, remove, and drain on paper towel. Alternatively, arrange the rice balls on an oiled baking sheet, brush gently with olive oil, and bake for about 10 minutes at 400°F until crisp and golden brown. Serve hot, with a little tomato sauce for dipping, or salad.

Serves 4–6

vitello tonnato
veal in milanese sauce

see variations page 79

This veal and tuna dish tastes better with homemade mayonnaise. Whisk 1 egg until pale yellow. Gradually add 1/2 cup each of sunflower seed oil and extra-virgin olive oil in a thin, slow, steady stream. Gradually, the oil and egg will emulsify and acquire a thick, smooth texture. Add 1 tablespoon lemon juice and season to taste.

2 1/4 lbs veal fillet joint
for the marinade
1 bottle dry white wine (less 1 glass, to be set aside)
1 onion, peeled and sliced
1 carrot, scraped and sliced
4 whole cloves
3 bay leaves, chopped
sea salt and freshly ground black pepper
2 1/3 cups veal or chicken stock (pages 22–3)
for the sauce
1 1/4 cups thick homemade mayonnaise

8 oz. canned tuna in olive oil, drained and flaked
sea salt and freshly ground black pepper
2 handfuls capers, rinsed, dried, and chopped
the reserved glass of wine
for the garnish
black olives
capers
gherkins
lemon slices
chopped fresh parsley

Lay the veal in a deep bowl. Mix together the marinade ingredients and pour over the veal. Let stand overnight. Remove the meat from the marinade, wrap it tightly in cheesecloth, tie it up tight, and lay in a deep saucepan. Pour the marinade and stock over the veal. Simmer slowly, covered, for about 1 1/2 hours or until the meat is cooked through. Let the meat cool in its marinade, then remove and unwrap. Slice the veal very thinly onto a large, flat platter. Mix the sauce ingredients together and coat the sliced meat with sauce. Garnish the platter and serve at once, or chill until required.

Serves 6

crostini di fegato alla toscana
tuscan crostini with liver paté

see variations page 80

This is the original classic Tuscan recipe for crostini, reputedly from the Medici kitchens, which some say is the original recipe for pâté. It has given rise to a plethora of other crostini recipes.

1/2 onion, finely chopped
1 carrot, finely chopped
1 stalk celery, finely chopped
1 tbsp. finely chopped fresh parsley
3 tbsp. olive oil
3 tbsp. butter
1 chicken liver, trimmed and washed carefully

1/4 lb. calf's liver, trimmed, washed and dried
2 tbsp. dry white wine
1 heaping tbsp. tomato paste
4 tbsp. hot water or stock
sea salt and freshly ground black pepper
1 oz. capers, rinsed and finely chopped
4 or 8 thin slices crusty bread

In a large skillet, sauté the onion, carrot, celery, and parsley in the olive oil and half the butter. Cook until soft, then add both livers. Stir and add the wine. Evaporate the wine over high heat for about 2 minutes, then add the tomato paste diluted in 2 tablespoons hot water or stock. Season to taste, then add the remaining water or stock, cover, and simmer for 20 minutes. Remove from the heat, lift the livers from the sauce, and mince or process them until smooth. Return the processed livers to the pan and stir in the remaining butter and all the capers. Heat through, then remove from the heat, but keep warm. Spread lightly toasted, warm bread slices generously with pâté and serve.

Serves 6

minestrone

minestrone

see variations page 81

Minestrone means "big soup" — it is designed to fill you up. The vegetables used can vary according to personal taste and availability, but this is the classic recipe.

1/2 lb. fresh, dried, or canned borlotti beans
1 onion, peeled and chopped finely
4 tbsp. olive oil
2 tbsp. chopped fresh flat-leaf parsley
3/4 lb. chopped green leaf vegetables (spinach, cabbage, swiss chard, lettuce, turnip tops)
2 zucchini, cubed   *mushroom*

1 potato, peeled and cubed
1 carrot, scraped and cubed
scant 1/2 lb. short stubby pasta, such as cannolicchi, avemarie, or tiny maccheroni
sea salt and freshly ground black pepper
extra-virgin olive oil, to serve
freshly grated Parmesan cheese, to serve

If using fresh or dried beans, soak them in cold water. Dried beans need to be soaked overnight; fresh beans take less time. Drain the beans, then cook in fresh water for 5 minutes. Drain and rinse, then cook slowly in fresh water until tender. Do not salt the water until the beans are tender, or the skins will toughen. They will be ready to add to soup when cooked, but not falling apart. If using canned beans, drain and rinse in cold water before adding to the soup. Next, fry onion in olive oil for about 5 minutes, in the bottom of a pot large enough to take all the ingredients. Add parsley and all the vegetables, stir, and cook for 5 minutes. Pour in the cooked beans and water to cover. Simmer gently for about 60 minutes, stirring frequently and topping off with liquid when necessary. Add more water if necessary to maintain enough liquid to cook the vegetables. Add pasta when vegetables are cooked. Season with salt and pepper. Serve hot as soon as pasta is tender, or cool and serve at room temperature or even chilled. Dress each serving with olive oil and Parmesan.

Serves 6

zuppa di pesce
fish soup

see variations page 82

This is the easiest recipe for making a really Italian-tasting fish soup. You can add mussels, shrimp, and all manner of fish or seafood if you wish, although the basic recipe calls only for filleted white fish, which makes it really easy to eat. The bread soaks up all the flavors and juices of the fish and is eaten at the end, once all the fish is gone.

3 1/2 lbs. filleted fish of various kinds (cod, monkfish, haddock, etc.)
1/2 cup olive oil
5 cloves garlic, finely chopped
1 dried red chile pepper
4 tbsp. chopped fresh flat-leaf parsley
3 handfuls cherry tomatoes, halved

sea salt and freshly ground black pepper
1 1/4 cups white wine
scant 1 cup fish stock
12 thin slices ciabatta bread, toasted
1 clove garlic, peeled and left whole
2 tbsp. extra-virgin olive oil, to serve
2 tbsp. chopped fresh flat-leaf parsley, to serve

Prepare the fish first. Trim carefully, wash, and pat dry. Heat the oil gently in a deep saucepan with garlic, chile pepper, parsley, and tomatoes, for about 5 minutes. Add the fish and stir. Season with salt and pepper and pour in the wine and fish stock. Cover tightly and simmer very gently for about 15 minutes.

Rub the toasted bread with garlic, then line a large, wide bowl with bread slices. Pour the hot fish mixture all over bread, drizzle with a little olive oil, sprinkle with a final dusting of parsley, and serve at once.

Serves 6

zuppa di fave bianche
white bean soup

see variations page 83

This fava (or broad) bean soup is one of the simplest soups and absolutely delicious as long as the dried beans have not become stale and the olive oil is really flavorsome. Use skinless dried beans, which are creamy white in color.

1 lb. dried white fava or broad beans,
   rinsed thoroughly
4 pints cold water

sea salt
6 tbsp. olive oil
freshly ground black pepper, to serve

Put the beans into the saucepan in which they will be cooked. Cover with approximately 4 pints of cold water. Let stand overnight. In the morning, simmer the beans in their soaking water for about 45–55 minutes, until reduced to a smooth purée. Add more water if the purée appears to be drying out too much. Stir frequently and season with salt to taste. When the beans have disintegrated into a smooth creamy texture, stir in the olive oil and serve immediately, sprinkled with freshly ground black pepper.

Serves 6

variations

pane con la farina di polenta
bread with polenta flour

see base recipe page 25

pan di polenta con uvetta *(polenta bread with raisins)*
Prepare basic recipe, kneading a handful of golden raisins (soaked in hot water for 20 minutes to allow them to swell, then drained) into the dough with the salt and oil.

pan di polenta coi pinoli *(polenta bread with pine nuts)*
Prepare basic recipe, kneading a handful of pine nuts into the dough with the salt and oil.

pan di polenta con ricotta *(polenta bread with ricotta)*
Prepare basic recipe. When the dough has risen, spread it out flat and cover with a thin layer of fresh ricotta. Sprinkle with salt and pepper, fold in half, and let rise again for about 30 minutes before stroking the surface with oil and water and baking.

pan di polenta con rosmarino e salvia *(polenta bread with rosemary & sage)*
Prepare basic recipe, kneading a generous handful of washed, coarsely chopped fresh rosemary and sage leaves into the dough with the salt and oil.

pan di polenta con pomodori secchi *(sun-dried tomato polenta bread)*
Prepare basic recipe, kneading 2 handfuls of coarsely chopped sun-dried tomatoes into the dough with the salt and oil.

variations

focaccia
focaccia

see base recipe page 26

focaccia al rosmarino *(focaccia with rosemary)*
Prepare basic recipe. Before baking, after oiling and salting the dough, sprinkle
with chopped fresh rosemary leaves.

focaccia con cipolla rossa *(focaccia with red onion)*
Prepare basic recipe. Before baking, cover the oiled and salted focaccia with a thin
layer of finely sliced red onion, brush with a little more oil, and bake as normal.

focaccia alle olive *(focaccia with olives)*
Prepare basic recipe, kneading a handful of chopped black or green olives into the
dough before leaving it to rise. Just before baking, push about 12 whole pitted
olives into the dough.

focaccia al pomodoro *(focaccia with cherry tomatoes)*
Prepare basic recipe. Just before baking, after oiling and salting the dough, scatter
about 15 cherry tomatoes over the surface. Brush the tomatoes with a little bit
of olive oil and bake as normal.

focaccia con patate *(focaccia with potatoes)*
Prepare basic recipe. While the dough rises, parboil 2 peeled medium potatoes,
then slice thinly. Before oiling, salting, and baking, cover the surface completely
with the sliced potatoes. Drizzle with oil, sprinkle with salt, and bake as normal.

variations

la panzanella
tuscan bread salad

see base recipe page 29

panzanella col pesce *(tuscan bread salad with fish)*
Prepare basic recipe, adding some lightly grilled fillets of red mullet or hake,
taking care not to break the fish up too much.

panzanella col tonno *(tuscan bread salad with tuna)*
Prepare basic recipe, adding some canned tuna in olive oil, carefully drained,
to the salad for extra protein and flavor. A few finely chopped canned
anchovy fillets will enhance the flavor of the tuna.

panzanella con le cozze *(tuscan bread salad with mussels)*
Prepare basic recipe, adding about 2 ounces cooked and shelled fresh
mussels to the salad. Use the strained, cooled, cooking liquid to soak
the bread.

panzanella con le olive nere *(tuscan bread salad with black olives)*
Prepare basic recipe, adding about 20 large black olives, pitted and coarsely
chopped, to the salad before dressing.

panzanella col pollo *(tuscan bread salad with chicken)*
Prepare basic recipe. Grill 2 skinless chicken breasts until cooked through and
well browned. Cool and slice into strips. Mix into the salad just before serving.

variations

insalata di asparagi e prosciutto di parma
asparagus & parma ham salad

see base recipe page 30

insalata di melone e prosciutto di parma *(melon & parma ham salad)*
Instead of basic recipe, wrap fresh melon chunks in Parma ham and serve
sprinkled with the balsamic vinegar and freshly ground black pepper.

insalata di fichi e prosciutto di parma *(fig & parma ham salad)*
Instead of basic recipe, wrap quartered, peeled fresh figs in Parma ham and
serve sprinkled with the balsamic vinegar and freshly ground black pepper.

insalata di mozzarelline e speck *(mozzarella & speck salad)*
Instead of basic recipe, wrap small balls of mozzarella (mozzarelline) in thin
slices of Speck (smoked, cured, air-dried ham). Arrange on a platter with lettuce
leaves and sprinkle with balsamic vinegar and freshly ground black pepper.

insalata di mozzarelline con la rucola *(mozzarella balls & arugula salad)*
Instead of basic recipe, wrap small balls of mozzarella in Parma ham. Arrange on a
bed of arugula, dressed with balsamic vinegar, extra-virgin olive oil, salt, and pepper.
Serve sprinkled with more balsamic vinegar and black pepper.

insalata di carciofini e prosciutto di parma *(baby artichoke & parma ham salad)*
Instead of basic recipe, wrap small artichoke hearts preserved in oil in thin slices
of Parma ham. Arrange on a bed of lettuce and sprinkle with balsamic and black
pepper. Add bits of mozzarella to salad (optional).

variations

rotolini di bresaola con la rucola
cured beef rolls with arugula

see base recipe page 33

bresaola con la rucola *(cured beef & arugula platter)*
Omit Parmesan, lemon, and chives. Arrange the bresaola on a platter and
cover with arugula. Whisk together olive oil and balsamic vinegar, season
with salt and pepper, and drizzle over dish.

bresaola con la cipolla rossa *(cured beef & red onion platter)*
Omit arugula, lemon, and chives. Arrange the bresaola on a platter and
cover with thinly sliced red onion. Whisk the olive oil with balsamic vinegar,
season, and drizzle over the dish. Serve the platter with chopped chives
scattered on top.

bresaola con la robiola *(cured beef & cream cheese platter)*
Omit lemon and chives. Wrap the bresaola around spoonfuls of creamy
cheese such as robiola and arrange on top of the arugula. Scatter with
Parmesan shavings. Whisk the olive oil with balsamic vinegar, season, and
drizzle over the dish.

bresaola con pompelmo rosa *(cured beef & pink grapefruit platter)*
Omit arugula, Parmesan, lemon, and chives. Arrange the bresaola on a
platter and cover with fresh pink grapefruit segments. Remove any excess
juice. Whisk olive oil with balsamic vinegar, season, and drizzle over dish.

variations

insalata di finocchio, salame e olive

fennel, salami & olive salad

see base recipe page 34

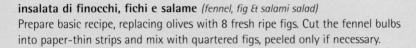

insalata di finocchi, fichi e salame *(fennel, fig & salami salad)*
Prepare basic recipe, replacing olives with 8 fresh ripe figs. Cut the fennel bulbs
into paper-thin strips and mix with quartered figs, peeled only if necessary.

insalata di cavolo, salame e olive *(white cabbage, salami & olive salad)*
Prepare basic recipe, replacing the fennel with half a white cabbage, very finely
shredded (as for coleslaw).

insalata di indivia, salame e olive *(endive, salami & olive salad)*
Prepare basic recipe, replacing the fennel with 8 heads of very finely shredded
Belgian endive.

insalata di pomodori verdi, salame e olive *(green tomato, salami & olive salad)*
Prepare basic recipe, replacing the fennel with 8 medium-sized, sliced, seeded,
very firm, and barely red tomatoes.

insalata di melone verde, salame e olive *(green melon, salami & olive salad)*
Prepare basic recipe, replacing the fennel with 14 ounces ripe but firm green
melon (such as honeydew), sliced very thinly.

variations

insalata di riso
rice salad

see base recipe page 37

pomodori ripieni d'insalata di riso *(rice salad-stuffed tomatoes)*
Prepare basic recipe. Cut the tops off ripe beefsteak tomatoes and scoop out
the seeds. Sprinkle inside with salt and turn over to drain for 30 minutes. Fill
tomatoes with rice salad, replace tops, arrange on a platter, and serve at once.

insalata di riso con le barbabietole e gamberetti *(beet & shrimp rice salad)*
Omit all ingredients except rice and dressing. Mix drained, warm rice with
2 cubed and peeled boiled beets, 7 ounces peeled cooked shrimp, and
4 chopped scallions. Mix with dressing. Serve at once.

insalata di riso con capperi e pomodorini *(caper & cherry tomato rice salad)*
Prepare basic recipe, replacing the potato, eggs, and anchovies with
2 or 3 handfuls of halved cherry tomatoes. Double the quantity of capers.

insalata di riso al tonno *(tuna rice salad)*
Prepare basic recipe, replacing the eggs and anchovies with canned or fresh
(cooked) tuna, flaked.

insalata di riso con i pinoli e le olive verdi *(pine nut & olive rice salad)*
Prepare basic recipe, omitting the eggs, anchovies, and capers. Double or triple
the olives (using only green olives) and add toasted pine nuts.

insalata di tonno e fagioli
tuna & bean salad

see base recipe page 38

insalata di gamberetti e fagioli *(shrimp & bean salad)*
Prepare basic recipe, replacing the tuna with cooked shrimp, red onion with a little chopped scallion, and vinegar with lemon juice.

insalata di cannellini con le cozze *(mussel & cannellini bean salad)*
Prepare basic recipe, replacing the tuna with about 25 cooked, shelled mussels. Omit the onion. Replace the vinegar with lemon juice.

insalata di tonno e ceci *(tuna & garbanzo bean salad)*
Prepare basic recipe, replacing the beans with drained canned chickpeas.

insalata di ceci e gamberetti *(prawn & garbanzo bean salad)*
Prepare basic recipe, replacing the beans with chickpeas, tuna with cooked shrimp, red onion with chopped scallion, and vinegar with lemon juice.

variations

insalata di frutti di mare
seafood salad

see base recipe page 41

insalata di calamari con peperoncino fresco *(squid salad with fresh chile)*
Prepare basic recipe, omitting all seafood but squid and doubling the
amount of squid. Replace black pepper with very finely chopped fresh chile
pepper. Mix the boiled squid with the dressing and serve with lemon slices.

insalata di gamberetti *(shrimp salad)*
Prepare basic recipe, omitting all seafood but the shrimp. Cook 14 ounces
peeled, deveined shrimp, mix with the dressing, garnish with lemon slices,
and serve.

insalata di calamari e pancetta *(squid & pancetta salad)*
Prepare basic recipe, omitting all seafood but the squid. Boil double the
amount of squid until tender, then drain. Slice and mix with 3 ounces fried
pancetta cubes, then mix with the dressing and garnish with lemon slices.

insalata di capesante *(scallop salad)*
Prepare basic recipe, replacing all the seafood with 12 large scallops. Sear
the scallops with a little oil for 2–3 minutes per side, slice horizontally, and
mix with the dressing. Garnish with lemon slices to serve.

variations

insalata caprese
tricolor salad

see base recipe page 42

caprese con avocado *(tricolor salad with avocado)*
Prepare basic recipe, adding 1 ripe avocado, sliced.

caprese con prosciutto di parma *(tricolor salad with parma ham)*
Prepare basic recipe, adding some thin strips of freshly sliced Parma ham.

caprese con peperoni al forno *(tricolor salad with roasted salami)*
Prepare basic recipe, adding roasted peppers preserved in olive oil or roast them yourself in a medium-hot oven or under a broiler.

caprese con melanzane alla griglia *(tricolor salad with grilled eggplant)*
Prepare basic recipe, adding a few slices of grilled eggplant to make the salad considerably more substantial. Use grilled eggplant preserved in olive oil or slice and grill it yourself. Before grilling, sprinkle slices with sea salt and place in a colander to drain, covered with a weighted plate. After an hour, rinse, dry, and brush with a little olive oil.

caprese con carciofini *(tricolor salad with artichoke hearts)*
Prepare basic recipe, adding a few chopped, drained, oil-marinated artichoke hearts.

variations

insalata di rucola, pere e parmigiano
arugula, pear & parmesan salad

see base recipe page 45

insalata di rucola, pesche e parmigiano *(arugula, peach & parmesan salad)*
Prepare basic recipe, replacing the pears with slices of firm, carefully peeled peaches.

insalata di rucola, pesche noci e parmigiano *(arugula, nectarine & parmesan salad)*
Prepare basic recipe, replacing the pears with slices of unpeeled, firm nectarines.

insalata di rucola, mango verde e parmigiano *(arugula, green mango & parmesan salad)*
Prepare basic recipe, replacing the pears with sliced unripe mangoes for an Asian twist to this otherwise very Italian salad.

insalata di rucola, pomodorini e parmigiano *(arugula, cherry tomato & parmesan salad)*
Prepare basic recipe, replacing the pears with quartered cherry tomatoes or cubed larger tomatoes for a less sweet salad.

insalata di rucola, pere e pecorino *(arugula, pear & pecorino salad)*
Prepare basic recipe, replacing the Parmesan with pecorino.

insalata di pomodori e olive con crema di olive
tomato & olive salad with olive paste

see base recipe page 46

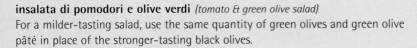

insalata di pomodori e olive verdi *(tomato & green olive salad)*
For a milder-tasting salad, use the same quantity of green olives and green olive
pâté in place of the stronger-tasting black olives.

insalata di pomodori e capperi *(tomato & caper salad)*
For a different-tasting salad, use capers in place of the olives. Dress the salad
without the olive pâté, using olive oil and lemon juice instead.

insalata di pomodori, olive e peperoni *(tomato, olive & pepper salad)*
This salad works very well when half the quantity of tomatoes is exchanged
for fresh red and green peppers, cut into small cubes.

insalata di pomodori a olive all'aglio *(tomato & olive salad with garlic)*
To make the salad taste subtly of garlic, omit the red onions and use 3 finely
minced cloves of garlic, stirred into the dressing.

insalata di pomodori, olive e sedano *(tomato, olive & celery salad)*
Adding a few chopped stalks of celery to this salad changes the flavor and adds
lots of extra crunch.

variations

carpaccio di zucchini
raw zucchini salad

see base recipe page 49

carpaccio di carciofi *(raw artichoke salad)*
Prepare basic recipe, replacing salted zucchini slices with thin slices of
carefully cleaned and prepared artichoke. Replace the parsley with freshly
chopped mint.

carpaccio di funghi *(raw mushroom salad)*
Prepare basic recipe, replacing the salted zucchini slices with 1/2 pound
of thinly sliced mushrooms.

carpaccio di finocchi *(raw fennel salad)*
Prepare basic recipe, replacing the salted zucchini slices with 1/2 pound
of thinly sliced fennel bulbs.

carpaccio di zucchine e carote *(raw carrot salad)*
Prepare basic recipe, adding paper-thin slices of 2 carrots to the salted
zucchini slices.

carpaccio di finocchi e mele *(raw apple & fennel salad)*
Prepare basic recipe, replacing the salted zucchini slices with 1/2 pound
of thinly sliced fennel bulbs and 2 small tart apples, peeled and thinly sliced.

carciofi alla romana
baked artichokes

see base recipe page 50

carciofi al prosciutto di parma *(baked artichokes & parma ham)*
Prepare the basic recipe, omitting garlic, mint, and lemon peel. Fill the centers
with chopped Parma ham, chopped fresh flat-leaf parsley, salt, and pepper.

carciofi alla piemontese *(piedmontese-style baked artichokes)*
Prepare basic recipe, omitting garlic, mint, and lemon peel. Spread the centers
with butter, salt, pepper, and a generous amount of freshly grated Parmesan.

carciofi alla fiorentina *(florentine-style baked artichokes)*
Prepare basic recipe, omitting wine, mint, and lemon peel. Fill centers
with chopped garlic and finely chopped pancetta. Braise with water and
oil until tender.

carciofi al pomodoro *(baked artichokes with tomatoes)*
Instead of basic recipe, braise the artichokes with chopped onions and
chopped canned tomatoes until softened all the way through. Season and
sprinkle with freshly chopped parsley and basil to serve.

bruschetta di carciofi *(baked artichokes on bruschetta)*
Prepare basic recipe. Serve cooked artichokes on garlicky bruschetta (toasted
crusty bread rubbed with garlic and drizzled with a little olive oil), garnished
with a few lettuce leaves.

variations

arancini di riso
rice croquettes

see base recipe page 53

arancini con porcini *(mushroom rice croquettes)*
Prepare basic recipe, omitting peas, mushrooms, and Parma ham. Soak
1 1/2 ounces dried porcini mushrooms in a small bowl of hot water for
about 1 hour or until softened. Drain carefully and discard the liquid. Toss
the mushrooms in a pan with 1 tablespoon butter until cooked through. Mix
cooked mushrooms into cold risotto and continue as in main recipe.

arancini con emmenthal *(emmenthal rice croquettes)*
Prepare basic recipe, replacing mozzarella with small cubes of Emmenthal.

arancini con salame *(salami rice croquettes)*
Prepare basic recipe, using chopped salami instead of Parma ham.

arancini al ragú *(rice croquettes with bolognese sauce)*
Prepare basic recipe, omitting peas, mushrooms, and Parma ham from the
rice balls. Insert a teaspoonful of ragú alla bolognese (page 89) as well as the
mozzarella into the center of each rice ball before rolling in flour, beaten
egg, and bread crumbs. Fry or bake as in main recipe.

variations

vitello tonnato
veal in milanese sauce

see base recipe page 54

pollo tonnato *(chicken in milanese sauce)*
Prepare basic recipe, omitting veal and marinade. Use the sauce to cover gently poached skinless chicken breasts.

tonnato alle olive *(milanese veal with olives)*
Prepare basic recipe. Mix two handfuls of coarsely chopped, pitted black and green olives into the sauce before serving.

tonnato di pesce *(fish in milanese sauce)*
Prepare basic recipe, omitting veal and marinade. Poach thick fillets of haddock or cod until cooked through, then serve with a thin coating of sauce. Offer the rest separately in a sauceboat.

tonnato di patate *(potatoes with milanese sauce)*
Prepare basic recipe, omitting veal and marinade. Use the tonnato sauce to dress freshly boiled and peeled new potatoes or as a filling for baked potatoes.

maiale tonnato *(pork in milanese sauce)*
Prepare basic recipe, replacing the veal with fillet of pork.

variations

crostini di fegato alla toscana
tuscan crostini with pâté

see base recipe page 57

crostini di fegato con uova di quaglia *(tuscan crostini with quail's egg)*
Prepare basic recipe. After spreading pâté on warm toast, top each one with
a quail's egg fried in butter until just set.

crostini di fegato con le cipolle rosse *(tuscan crostini with red onion)*
Prepare basic recipe. Thinly spread warm pâté on warm toast, then top each
one with a tiny spoonful of warm, caramelized red onions.

crostini di fegato col balsamico *(tuscan crostini with balsamic vinegar)*
Prepare basic recipe. After spreading the pâté on warm toast, drizzle a little
good-quality balsamic vinegar over each slice.

crostini di fegato ai funghi *(tuscan crostini with mushrooms)*
Prepare basic recipe. After spreading the pâté on warm toast, top each slice
with a small spoonful of warm, thinly sliced, cooked mushrooms.

crostini di fegato d'anatra *(tuscan crostini with duck pâté)*
Prepare basic recipe, but for a much richer pâté, use duck livers instead
of the chicken and veal.

minestrone
minestrone

see base recipe page 58

minestrone alla zucca *(minestrone with pumpkin)*
To make a minestrone with a lovely orange color, replace the greens with the
same weight of diced, peeled pumpkin or butternut squash. Cook it until
softened before continuing with the remaining ingredients.

minestrone di patate *(potato minestrone)*
Prepare basic recipe, but for a very filling minestrone, replace the zucchini,
potato, and carrot with cubed potatoes.

minestrone di ceci *(minestrone with chickpeas)*
Prepare basic recipe, replacing the borlotti beans with same amount
of canned chickpeas, drained and rinsed well before adding to soup.

minestrone con lenticchie *(minestrone with green lentils)*
Prepare basic recipe, replacing the borlotti beans with lentils. Follow the
package instructions to cook the lentils before adding to the soup.

minestrone al riso *(minestrone with rice)*
Prepare basic recipe, replacing the pasta with the same amount
of long-grain rice.

variations

zuppa di pesce
fish stew

see base recipe page 61

zuppa di cozze *(mussel stew)*
Prepare basic recipe, replacing the fish with 3 1/2 pounds mussels, carefully scrubbed clean and rinsed repeatedly in several changes of cold water. Omit fish stock, as mussels will create their own liquid. Reduce simmering time by about 5 minutes and shake the pan occasionally to ensure all mussels open.

zuppa di vongole *(clam stew)*
Prepare basic recipe, replacing the fish with 5 pounds medium-sized clams (such as cherrystones or vongole veraci), washed and scrubbed clean. Use half the amount of fish stock, as the clams will create their own liquid. Mix once or twice to help the clams open up. Simmer until all clams are open.

zuppa di pesce passata *(smooth fish soup)*
Prepare basic recipe. After simmering, push it through a food mill, or whiz in a food processor, until smooth and velvety. Pour over the garlic-scented toasted bread and serve.

variations

zuppa di fave bianche
white bean soup

see base recipe page 62

zuppa di fave e maiale *(pork & bean soup)*
Prepare basic recipe. Remove the meat from 2 small pork chops and chop
coarsely. Fry with a clove of garlic in a little olive oil until very tender,
basting with a little wine. Stir into the soup and serve.

zuppa di fave e piselli *(pea & bean soup)*
Prepare basic recipe, but replace half the beans with dried peas.

zuppa di cannellini con fontina *(cannellini soup with fontina cheese)*
Instead of basic recipe, replace the broad beans with cannellini beans. Soak
in water, then drain. Cook in about 2 pints of milk. Simmer gently until the
beans start falling apart. Bring to a boil, remove from heat, and mix in about
1 cup of cubed fontina cheese until melted. Serve at once.

zuppa d'orzo *(pearl barley soup)*
Use barley instead of the broad beans and proceed with the recipe as before.
Simmer for about an hour and serve hot, with freshly grated Parmesan
offered separately.

primi piatti: pasta

first course: pasta

It is almost impossible to think about Italian food without pasta, a subject dear to every Italian heart, whether it is fresh egg pasta or dried durum wheat pasta. These recipes are all perfect for when you're expecting a crowd.

pasta con la ricotta
pasta with ricotta

see variations page 108

One of the simplest pasta sauces, very easy to make and fresh and delicious. Make sure the ricotta is as fresh as possible for the best possible results. Using ewe's milk ricotta will give the sauce a stronger flavor.

1 lb. pasta of your choice
sea salt
8 oz. ricotta
4 tbsp. freshly grated Parmesan,
    plus extra to serve

freshly ground black pepper
2 tbsp. extra-virgin olive oil

Bring a large pot of salted water to a rolling boil. Meanwhile, mix the ricotta with a little salt and the Parmesan and pepper. Slacken the sauce slightly with a little boiling water from the pot to make sure you can distribute it smoothly through the pasta. Add the pasta to the boiling water and stir, return to a boil, and cook until al dente, then drain and mix with the ricotta. Drizzle with the olive oil just before serving.

Serves 6

pasta al pomodoro
pasta with tomato sauce

see variations page 109

This is the basic tomato sauce from which so many favorites are created. As with all recipes that rely on the quality of a few ingredients for the best results, this sauce needs good olive oil and the sweetest tomatoes for the most perfect flavor. If you wish, you may offer freshly grated Parmesan at the table.

1 medium-sized onion
1 large carrot
1 large stalk celery
4 tbsp. extra-virgin olive oil

1 lb. skinned and seeded fresh tomatoes, or
1 (14-oz.) can tomatoes, with juice
sea salt and freshly ground black pepper
1 lb. pasta of your choice

Peel and chop the onion very finely. Scrape and wash the carrot, then chop finely. Finally, wash the celery, tear away strings, and chop finely (a few celery leaves would also be welcome). Pour the oil into a heavy-bottomed saucepan and add the chopped vegetables. Fry together very gently and slowly until the vegetables are soft and the onion is transparent. Only at this point, add the tomatoes and stir thoroughly. Cover and simmer for about 30 minutes, stirring regularly. Season with salt and pepper to taste. (If you wish to add herbs, do so at the end once the sauce is cooked through.)

Bring a large pot of salted water to a rolling boil, add pasta, and stir. Cook until al dente, then drain and return to the pot. Add the sauce, toss together, and serve in a warmed serving dish or bowl or on individual warmed plates.

Serves 6

pasta al ragú alla bolognese
pasta with bolognese sauce

see variations page 110

This is the classic, original recipe for the rich meaty sauce from the city of Bologna. It uses only a little tomato paste and several different kinds of finely chopped meat, which give the sauce a stewlike texture. Offer freshly grated Parmesan at the table.

1/4 lb. boneless pork loin
1/4 lb. boneless beef
1/4 lb. Parma ham
1/2 cup (1 stick) butter
1 carrot, finely chopped
1 stalk celery, finely chopped
1 onion, finely chopped

2 1/2 oz. pancetta or bacon, finely chopped
1 heaping tbsp. tomato paste diluted with
    1/2 cup hot water
sea salt and freshly ground black pepper
1 1/2 ladles hot broth or water
14 oz. fresh or dried pasta of your choice
freshly grated Parmesan, to serve

Finely chop the meats together with a knife. In a large heavy-based pan, melt half the butter, then add the vegetables and pancetta or bacon and cook for 5–6 minutes, stirring over medium heat. Add the chopped meats and stir together to brown. Add the diluted tomato paste. Season with salt and pepper. Stir thoroughly, cover, and let simmer very slowly for about 2 hours. Watch that it does not dry out; stir frequently and keep adding a little hot water or broth as needed. After about 2 hours, when the meat is tender, add the remaining butter and stir. Remove from the heat. The sauce can be used now, but it improves with standing and reheating. To serve, bring a large pot of salted water to a rolling boil, stir in the pasta, cook until al dente, then drain and return to the pot. Add the warm sauce, toss, and transfer to a serving dish or individual plates to serve.

Serves 6

pasta alla carbonara

pasta with carbonara sauce

see variations page 111

This classic pasta dish is traditionally served with either spaghetti or bucatini. It relies on the flavor of the pancetta and plenty of freshly ground black pepper for the best results.

14 oz. bucatini or spaghetti
sea salt
7 oz. pancetta, guanciale, or best-quality
   bacon, cubed

3 eggs, beaten
5 tbsp. grated pecorino or Parmesan
freshly ground black pepper

Bring a large pot of salted water to a boil. Add the pasta and stir thoroughly. Replace the lid and return to a boil. Remove or adjust the lid when the water is boiling again. While the pasta is cooking, fry the pancetta in a very hot skillet until crisp and running freely with fat. Beat the eggs in a bowl with the cheese and plenty of black pepper.

When the pasta is cooked al dente, drain and return to the pot. Immediately pour the egg mixture and pancetta over the pasta and stir everything together so that the eggs scramble and pull the dish together. The fat from the pancetta should sizzle and fry as it mingles with the pasta. Serve at once.

Serves 6

pasta primavera
pasta with spring vegetable sauce

see variations page 112

The word *primavera*, which means "spring" in Italian, is often used to identify various pasta dishes dressed with a vegetable-based sauce. There are many different versions of the basic recipe.

4 tbsp. olive oil
1 small red onion, peeled and chopped
1 carrot, scraped and chopped coarsely
2 small zucchini, topped and tailed and cubed
1 small green or red bell pepper, seeded
   and cubed
1 (16-oz.) can chopped tomatoes

2 tbsp. water
large pinch dried oregano
1/2 lb. cherry tomatoes, washed and halved
1 lb. pasta of your choice
sea salt and freshly ground black pepper
freshly grated Parmesan, to serve

Bring a large pot of salted water to a boil for the pasta. In a separate large pan on medium-high heat, heat the oil. Add the vegetables, stirring to coat with oil. Cook for about 10 minutes, stirring only occasionally, until the vegetables are just cooked. Turn off the heat, but keep the pan on the burner. Add the canned tomatoes to the vegetables, with the water to thin the sauce if necessary. Gently mix in the oregano and cherry tomatoes.

Meanwhile, add the pasta to the boiling water and cook until al dente. Drain the pasta and put into the pan with the vegetables. Adjust seasoning and mix together, adding a little more olive oil if necessary. Serve on a warmed serving dish or individual plates, sprinkled with a little freshly grated Parmesan.

Serves 6

pasta al pesto
pasta with pesto

see variations page 113

The word *pesto* is derived from the verb *pestare* meaning "to pound." The most popular and best-known pesto is the emerald green version from the region of Liguria that uses basil, garlic, and pine nuts. There are many other versions of this sauce that are perhaps not as well-known, but just as delicious, which use quite different ingredients. This is the classic recipe from the port city of Genoa.

2–4 large handfuls fresh basil leaves, washed
    but not bruised, dried carefully
1 large pinch kosher salt
2–3 cloves garlic, peeled and halved
1 generous handful pine nuts

2–6 tbsp. grated Parmesan or pecorino or
    half of each
about 1/2 cup best-quality olive oil
sea salt and freshly ground black pepper
1 lb. pasta of your choice

If using a mortar and pestle, put basil, salt, and garlic into the mortar and reduce to a smooth green purée with the pestle. (Remember to press basil leaves against the sides; do not bang downward. You want to purée them and not bruise them too much.) Add pine nuts and cheese and blend in. Then add the oil a little at a time, until the pesto has a smooth, creamy texture. Season with salt and pepper. If using a food processor, add the ingredients in the same order. Remember to taste as you go along and adjust quantities according to taste.

Bring a large pot of salted water to a rolling boil, add the pasta, and boil until al dente. Drain and return to the pot, saving a little of the cooking water. Add the pesto and mix together (add reserved cooking water to help distribute the pesto evenly and smoothly through the pasta if necessary), then transfer to a serving dish or individual plates to serve.

Serves 6

pasta al forno
pasta bake

see variations page 114

This is a simple baked pasta dish, using béchamel sauce, ham, and cheese. It is comfort food, perfect as an easy supper dish with a tossed salad.

14 oz. short pasta, such as penne
sea salt and freshly ground black pepper
2 1/4 cups béchamel sauce (page 100)

6 tbsp. freshly grated Parmesan
scant 1/2 lb. best-quality baked ham, chopped
3 tbsp. butter

Preheat oven to 400°F. Cook the pasta in plenty of boiling salted water until al dente. Drain the pasta and pour it back into the pot.

Meanwhile, gently heat the sauce and stir in 4 tablespoons Parmesan. Add three quarters of the sauce and the ham to the pasta. Mix gently. Grease a 10 x 12-inch ovenproof dish with half the butter. Pour in the dressed pasta. Cover with the remaining béchamel sauce and dot with the remaining butter. Sprinkle with the remaining cheese. Bake for about 15 minutes or until golden and bubbling. Remove from the oven, let rest for 5 minutes, and serve.

Serves 6

cannelloni ai funghi
mushroom cannelloni

see variations page 115

One of the best things about cannelloni is that they are so versatile and can be filled with almost anything (such as this mushroom filling) before being coated with sauce and baked. You can prepare it in advance and then bake just before serving.

9 oz. fresh lasagna noodle sheets
3 tbsp. olive oil
1 clove garlic, lightly crushed
3 small onions, peeled and chopped
1 lb. fresh mushrooms, cleaned and cubed
sea salt and freshly ground black pepper
4 oz. cream cheese

4 tbsp. melted butter
2 tbsp. butter
8 oz. canned tomatoes, drained, seeded, and coarsely chopped
1 scant cup light cream
5 oz. Parmesan, freshly grated
8 leaves fresh basil, washed and torn

Blanch the pasta sheets in boiling salted water for about 2 or 3 minutes and drop into cold water to prevent them sticking to each other. Set aside. To make the filling, heat the oil in a skillet, add garlic, and fry until browned. Remove and discard the garlic. Add onions and mushrooms to the pan and cook until softened. Season with salt and pepper, then gently stir in cream cheese. Brush melted butter over bottom and sides of a 10-inch-square ovenproof dish. Take a sheet of pasta, drain, and blot carefully. Place it flat on a board and add a tablespoon of filling. Roll up to make a cannellone and place into buttered dish. Repeat until pasta and filling have been used up. Melt butter in another pan, and add tomatoes. Simmer for about 10 minutes. Season with salt and pepper, add cream, half the Parmesan, and the basil. Remove from the heat and pour over filled cannelloni. Preheat the oven to 325°F. Sprinkle the cannelloni with remaining Parmesan and place in oven for 15–20 minutes, or until golden brown and bubbling hot. Let stand for 5 minutes before serving.
Serves 6

lasagna al forno
lasagna

see variations page 116

The amount of work required to make an authentic lasagna is really quite immense. As a result, most Italians choose to make lasagna for special occasions only. You could save one step by using a pound of ready-made dried or fresh lasagna.

for the pasta
2 cups all-purpose flour
6 extra-large eggs
for the sauce
1 large onion, peeled and finely chopped
1 large carrot, scraped and finely chopped
1 large stalk celery, finely chopped
2 tbsp. olive oil
3/4 lb. lean ground beef or veal
1/2 cup dry red wine
2 cups drained canned tomatoes

handful of dried porcini mushrooms, soaked in
    warm water for at least 1 hour
sea salt and freshly ground black pepper
for the béchamel
6 tbsp. butter
4 level tbsp. all-purpose flour
2 1/4 cups milk
sea salt
pinch grated nutmeg
1/4 lb. mozzarella, cubed
3 oz. Parmesan, freshly grated

Make the fresh pasta (page 20). Rest dough for about 30 minutes, then roll out until paper-thin and cut into rectangles about the size of your palm. Cook in boiling salted water in batches of about 3 at a time. As soon as the pasta rises to surface, remove with a slotted spoon and lay carefully on a clean, damp cloth or into bowl of cold water. If using store-bought pasta, check package for cooking instructions. To make the sauce, gently fry together onion, carrot, and celery for about 10 minutes, then add ground meat and cook until well browned. Add the wine and boil quickly for 2 minutes, then stir in the tomatoes. Return to a boil, then reduce heat to a low simmer and let cook slowly, stirring frequently, for about 90 minutes. Drain mushrooms, chop coarsely, and stir into sauce. Strain the mushroom

soaking water through a double layer of paper towel or cheesecloth, then add to sauce. Season, stir, and simmer another hour. To make béchamel, melt the butter in a saucepan. Add the flour and mix together into a smooth paste. Pour in the milk and whisk to prevent lumps forming. Add salt and nutmeg to taste and simmer gently for about 15 minutes, stirring constantly. When sauce is thick enough to coat the back of a spoon, remove from heat and cover the surface with a little cold water to prevent a skin from forming. Set aside. To assemble, cover bottom of a large 12 x 14-inch baking dish with a thin layer of béchamel, then a layer of pasta, then a layer of meat sauce, a scattering of mozzarella, a sprinkling of Parmesan, and another layer of béchamel. Top with a layer of pasta, and so on, until you have used up all the ingredients, finishing with a layer of béchamel and a final dusting of Parmesan. Let stand for 5–10 minutes, or longer, before baking for 30 minutes in a preheated oven at 400°F. When lasagna comes out of oven, let stand for 5 minutes before cutting.

Serves 6

ravioli con ripieno di ricotta

ricotta-stuffed ravioli

see variations page 117

This ricotta-filled ravioli is one of the simplest and most delicious of all the filled pasta recipes from Emilia-Romagna. It relies heavily on superior-quality ricotta.

7 oz. ricotta
pinch of grated nutmeg
salt and freshly ground black pepper
6 oz. Parmesan, freshly grated
6 eggs
1 cup all-purpose flour

1 cup fine semolina
1/4 teaspoon olive oil
1/2 cup plus 2 tbsp. butter
5 leaves fresh sage, rubbed gently between
    palms to release flavor

To make the filling, mix ricotta with nutmeg, salt and pepper, and half the Parmesan. Add 1 egg, stir, and set aside.

Tip flour and semolina onto the work surface and make a hollow in the center with your fist. Break the remaining 5 eggs into hollow. Mix eggs into flour, then begin to knead together. Add olive oil and knead until it is a smooth ball of elastic dough. With a rolling pin, roll dough out several times until fine, silky, and cool. Divide lengthwise into 2 1/2-inch-wide strips. Cover dough you are not using with a very slightly damp cloth to retain its moisture. Drop 3/4 teaspoonful of filling along one side of each strip, leaving a gap 2 fingers wide between each bit of filling, and a gap 1 finger wide at the front, leaving the other side (roughly half) of the pasta dough clear. Fold the clear strip in half toward you, encasing the filling. With a pastry cutter or an overturned glass, cut around each section of filling to make a crescent, cupping around the filling and pasta with just half the cutter. Seal the curved edge of each crescent with the prongs of a fork.

Continue until all the dough has been filled and cut. Line up all the finished ravioli on a clean, floured surface without touching each other until you cook them. Cover only with a clean soft napkin to avoid them getting dusty. Bring a large pot of salted water to a rolling boil. Drop in ravioli and boil until floating on the surface and tender. Remove with a slotted spoon and arrange in a warmed serving dish. Meanwhile, melt the butter with the sage leaves until warm and golden, not browned. When all ravioli are in the serving dish, pour on sage butter and mix carefully to distribute. Sprinkle with remaining cheese and serve at once.
Serves 6

tortellini in brodo
tortellini in broth

see variations page 118

This dish is part of the Christmas feast in many parts of Italy. The tortellini must be as small as possible and need a little practice to get absolutely right. They must not be overfilled and should be securely sealed so the filling does not escape into the broth.

1 large boiling fowl or capon, cleaned
3 carrots, washed, topped, and tailed
3 onions, halved
2 stalks celery, washed
2 tomatoes, washed and halved
2 cabbage leaves, washed
handful of fresh parsley, washed
4 quarts cold water
sea salt
3 tbsp. butter
1/4 lb. boneless pork loin, cubed

2 oz. turkey breast, cubed
1/4 lb. thick-cut mortadella, cubed
1/4 lb. thick-cut prosciutto crudo, cubed
2 eggs, beaten
sea salt and freshly ground black pepper
5 tbsp. freshly grated Parmesan
large pinch grated nutmeg
for the pasta
1 cup all-purpose flour
1 cup fine semolina
7 eggs

To make the broth, place the bird in a large pot with vegetables, water, and a little salt. Bring to a boil and let simmer gently for about 2 hours. Let cool in pot. Once cold, remove the bird and reserve for another dish. Strain the liquid through a fine sieve. Let stand, remove any fat that forms on top, and strain again. To make the filling, melt butter and fry pork and turkey for 10 minutes. Let cool. Mince by hand three times, or process once in a food processor, together with the prosciutto and mortadella. Stir in eggs, salt and pepper, Parmesan, and nutmeg. Mix thoroughly by hand, then set aside. Make pasta (page 20). It must be filled immediately in order to prevent drying out. You can use squares or circles of dough. For squares, work with one width of pasta at a time. Cut into equal-sized squares, the smaller

the better, though too small will be difficult to twist into shape. (I aim for 1 1/4-inch squares. Experiment with a few sizes to see what works best for you.) Drop 1/4 teaspoon of filling in the center of each square. Fold in half to make a triangle and seal edges closed. If needed, dab edges with a little cold water to help seal. Wind around the tip of your index finger, pressing the two outer ends of the triangle together firmly. Push off your finger and fold ring outwards to make tortellino shape. For circles, cut dough with a 2-inch biscuit cutter. Put 1/4 teaspoon of filling in center. Fold in half and hold between your middle and index finger. Wrap two extremities around the tip of your index finger. Push off your finger and turn half inside out to look like a little belly button. Lay the filled tortellini on a clean, floured board until required. Cover only with a clean napkin to avoid them getting dusty. To finish, bring broth to a gentle boil and add filled tortellini. Simmer until tortellini are cooked, then remove from heat, ladle into individual bowls or a soup tureen and serve.

Serves 6

rotolo di pasta alle barbabietole
pasta roll with beets

see variations page 119

A completely different interpretation of the concept of pasta, this is my own adaptation of a much more complicated dish. It is perfect for parties, as it can sit in hot water, once cooked, for up to 30 minutes if necessary. You can also freeze the roll, in the cloth, and cook it without defrosting. You'll need a sheet of cheesecloth or a large napkin to cook the pasta roll in — about 16 inches square. Make sure it is not saturated in fabric conditioner, as this would affect the flavor of the dish.

2 large beets, boiled
5 oz. mascarpone
2 tbsp. freshly grated Parmesan
large pinch ground cumin
sea salt and freshly ground black pepper

1 cup all-purpose flour
1 cup fine semolina
5 extra-large eggs
1/2 cup (1 stick) butter, melted
1 1/2 tsp. poppy seeds

To make filling, drain beets and let cool until warm. Peel and cube, then process or blend until completely smooth. Add mascarpone to make a smooth, quite thick purée. Stir in the Parmesan and cumin, then season to taste with salt and pepper. Set aside. Make pasta dough (page 20) using flour, semolina, and eggs. Knead, rest, then roll into a wide sheet with a rolling pin. The size of the sheet of pasta will depend on the size of your wrapping cloth and your fish kettle/pan. Allow enough fabric at each end of the roll for tying the cloth. Roll pasta evenly and as thinly as possible. Cut a neatly edged rectangle out of the sheet of pasta (any leftover scraps from around the edges can be chopped roughly once dry and used in soup). Spread the filling evenly and not too thickly (if you overfill the roll, the filling will just splurt out of the ends) over the pasta sheet and then roll pasta up like a jellyroll, making sure there is no air between each turn of the spiral. Wrap pasta roll tightly in your wrapping

cloth. You will end up with the long pasta roll wrapped in several turns of the cloth, with enough spare cloth at each end to tie tightly with string or rubber bands so that no water can get in under the cloth while the pasta cooks.

Bring a fish kettle or wide pan of salted water to a boil. Slide the wrapped roll into the water. Don't let it sag in the center as you place it in the water, which needs to be kept at a gentle boil for about 45 minutes to let the roll cook. Remove carefully and drain. Unwrap and lay on a board to slice with a very sharp knife. Arrange the slices on a plate and spoon melted butter, mixed with poppy seeds, on top.

Serves 6

variations

pasta con la ricotta
pasta with ricotta

see base recipe page 85

pasta con la ricotta al limone *(pasta with ricotta & lemon)*
Make the basic recipe, adding the grated zest of 1 lemon to the ricotta.

pasta con la ricotta al basilico *(pasta with ricotta & basil)*
Make the basic recipe, adding a handful of torn basil leaves to the ricotta.

pasta con la ricotta al prezzemolo *(pasta with ricotta & parsley)*
Make the basic recipe, adding a handful of finely chopped flat-leaf parsley
to the ricotta.

pasta con la ricotta e pomodorini *(pasta with ricotta & cherry tomatoes)*
Make the basic recipe, adding about 15 quartered cherry tomatoes to the
pasta and mix both together with the ricotta. Add 2 tablespoons of finely
chopped parsley to the mixed pasta.

pasta con la ricotta, capperi e olive *(pasta with ricotta, capers & olives)*
Make the basic recipe, adding a handful of washed and chopped capers and
one of chopped stoned green olives to the ricotta and pasta. Mix together
and proceed with basic recipe.

pasta al pomodoro
pasta with tomato sauce

see base recipe page 86

pasta al pomodoro all'aglio *(pasta with garlic & tomato sauce)*
Omit onion, carrot, and celery, and replace with 1–2 peeled cloves of garlic
(crushed for maximum flavor, or left whole for mildest flavor). Fry garlic
slowly in oil until pungent, then continue with basic recipe.

pasta al pomodoro con mozzarella *(pasta with tomato sauce & mozzarella)*
Prepare basic recipe, then add a ball of mozzarella, cubed, and let melt
before serving.

pasta al pomodoro con mascarpone *(pasta with tomato sauce & mascarpone)*
Prepare basic recipe, then add 2–3 tablespoons of mascarpone and toss
together to make a deliciously creamy sauce.

pasta al pomodoro con ricotta *(pasta with tomato sauce & ricotta)*
Prepare basic recipe, then toss with 2–3 tablespoons of ricotta and a handful
of Parmesan.

pasta al pomodoro con pancetta *(pasta with tomato sauce & pancetta)*
Prepare basic recipe, then toss with some crisply fried cubes of pancetta and
a handful of Parmesan.

variations

pasta al ragú alla bolognese

pasta with bolognese sauce

see base recipe page 89

ragú alla bolognese con fegatini e panna *(creamy chicken liver bolognese sauce)*
Prepare basic recipe. Fry about 1 cup cleaned and sliced chicken livers in butter
until cooked through. Stir into the sauce at end of cooking time along with a
few tablespoons of heavy cream.

ragú con macinata di manzo *(ground beef bolognese sauce)*
Prepare basic recipe, adding 1 pound ground beef to pan along with other
meats, and adding a can of chopped tomatoes to pan along with tomato paste.

ragú con macinata di maiale *(ground pork bolognese sauce)*
Prepare basic recipe, adding 1 pound ground pork to pan along with other
meats, and adding a can of chopped tomatoes to pan along with tomato paste.

ragú con salsiccie e funghi *(sausage & mushroom bolognese sauce)*
Prepare basic recipe, but replace pork, beef, and Parma ham with 4 Italian
sausages, skinned and crumbled, and a handful of dried porcini mushrooms,
soaked in water for 30 minutes, then drained and chopped.

ragú alla bolognese con piselli *(bolognese sauce with peas)*
Prepare basic recipe, adding some fresh or frozen and thawed peas to the sauce
about halfway through the cooking process.

variations

pasta alla carbonara
pasta with carbonara sauce

see base recipe page 90

pasta alla carbonara con zucchine *(pasta with carbonara sauce & zucchini)*
Prepare basic recipe, adding some cubed and separately sautéed zucchini to
the pancetta just before mixing into the pasta.

pasta alla carbonara con piselli *(pasta with carbonara sauce & peas)*
Prepare basic recipe, adding some fresh or frozen and thawed peas to braise
with the pancetta until cooked and tender. Then proceed as before.

pasta alla carbonara con prosciutto di parma *(pasta with carbonara sauce &
parma ham)*
Prepare basic recipe, substituting chopped Parma ham slices for the pancetta.

pasta alla carbonara con funghi *(pasta with carbonara sauce & mushrooms)*
Prepare basic recipe, adding some separately cooked mushrooms to the
skillet with the almost cooked pancetta.

pasta alla carbonara alla panna *(pasta with carbonara sauce & heavy cream)*
Prepare basic recipe, but for extra luxury, stir some heavy cream into beaten
eggs before mixing with pasta.

variations

pasta primavera
spring vegetable pasta

see base recipe page 93

pasta alla primavera con pisellini *(spring vegetable pasta with peas)*
Replace bell pepper with 2 cups fresh or frozen peas.

pasta alla primavera con peperone arrostito *(spring vegetable pasta with oven-roasted peppers)*
Prepare basic recipe, omitting bell pepper from sauce and roasting it separately instead. Cool, peel, and seed pepper, then stir into the sauce at the very end for a really sweet flavor.

pasta alla primavera con melanzane e pecorino *(spring vegetable pasta with eggplant)*
Replace carrot, zucchini, and pepper with a large cubed eggplant, salted and allowed to purge before rinsing and drying. Offer grated pecorino instead of Parmesan to serve.

pasta alla primavera con broccoli all'aglio *(spring vegetable pasta with garlic & broccoli)*
Replace the onion with 3 cloves of crushed garlic, and carrot, zucchini, and pepper with about 14 small florets of fresh broccoli.

pasta alla primavera con la panna *(spring vegetable pasta with cream)*
Stir about 4 tablespoons of heavy cream through the sauce at the end.

variations

pasta al pesto
pasta with pesto

see base recipe page 94

pesto piccante *(spicy pesto pasta)*
Prepare basic recipe, adding up to a whole fresh chile pepper, pounded to a
paste along with the other ingredients.

pesto con le noci *(walnut pesto pasta)*
Prepare basic recipe, replacing half the pine nuts with chopped
fresh walnuts.

pesto di mandorle *(almond pesto pasta)*
Prepare basic recipe, replacing pine nuts with 2 handfuls of blanched fresh
almonds, and replacing cheese with 2 chopped and seeded ripe tomatoes.

pesto di arugula *(arugula pesto pasta)*
Prepare the basic recipe replacing the basil with the same quantity of
arugula, washed and dried, then proceed as for the basic recipe.

variations

pasta al forno
pasta bake

see base recipe page 97

pasta al forno con pomodori *(pasta bake with tomatoes)*
Prepare basic recipe, scattering some chopped fresh tomatoes into the dish with the pasta.

pasta al forno al ragú *(pasta bake with bolognese sauce)*
Prepare basic recipe, omitting ham. Instead, mix about half the ragú (page 89) into the pasta with the béchamel sauce.

pasta al forno con gorgonzola e noci *(pasta bake with gorgonzola & walnuts)*
Prepare basic recipe, replacing the ham with chunks of Gorgonzola and some chopped walnuts.

pasta al forno con funghi *(pasta bake with mushrooms)*
Prepare basic recipe, adding some sautéed mushrooms to the pasta with the ham.

variations

cannelloni ai funghi
mushroom cannelloni

see base recipe page 98

cannelloni ripieni di ragú *(cannelloni stuffed with bolognese sauce)*
Replace mushroom filling with ragú alla bolognese (page 89). Replace the
tomato sauce with a cheesy béchamel sauce (stir 5 tablespoons freshly
grated Parmesan into the béchamel on page 100).

cannelloni al pesce *(fish cannelloni)*
Replace mushroom filling with flaked, cooked, white fish mixed with a little
béchamel sauce (page 100). Replace tomato sauce with béchamel sauce.

cannelloni di ricotta e spinaci *(cannelloni with ricotta & spinach)*
Prepare basic recipe, but replace mushroom filling with ricotta and spinach
filling (page 117). Replace tomato sauce with a cheesy béchamel (above).

cannelloni al radicchio *(cannelloni with chicory)*
Replace mushroom filling with radicchio leaves wilted in a little butter and
mixed with cubed Swiss cheese and ham. Replace the tomato sauce with a
cheesy béchamel (above).

cannelloni di cozze e pomodoro *(cannelloni with mussels & tomatoes)*
Omit mushroom filling. Stir 1 1/2 pounds cooked, drained, and shelled
mussels into béchamel sauce (page 100) and fill cannelloni. Replace tomato
sauce with pomodoro all'aglio (page 109).

variations

lasagne al forno
lasagne

see base recipe page 100

lasagne di verdure *(vegetable lasagne)*
Prepare basic recipe, replacing meat sauce with pomodoro sauce (page 86) and adding any cooked vegetables to the béchamel sauce.

lasagne di pesce *(fish lasagne)*
Prepare basic recipe, adding some flaked cooked white fish, cooked shrimp, and finely chopped fresh parsley to most of the béchamel. Top the finished lasagne with a layer of plain béchamel and a few dots of butter.

lasagne di spinaci e ricotta *(spinach & ricotta lasagne)*
Prepare basic recipe, adding another layer of cooked, well-drained, and finely chopped spinach mixed with equal amount of ricotta and seasoned with grated nutmeg, Parmesan, and 1 egg. Add a small handful of Parmesan to the béchamel sauce.

lasagne di pesto e patate *(pesto & potato lasagne)*
Prepare basic recipe, omitting the meat sauce and mozzarella. Mix pesto into béchamel. Use this sauce and boiled, thinly sliced potatoes to create layers between the pasta sheets, adding occasional drops of pesto. Finish with a layer of plain béchamel.

ravioli con ripieno di ricotta
ricotta-stuffed ravioli

see base recipe page 102

ravioli di ricotta e spinaci *(spinach-stuffed ravioli)*
Replace half the ricotta in the filling with finely chopped, cooked spinach.

ravioli di asparagi e mascarpone *(asparagus & mascarpone-stuffed ravioli)*
Prepare basic recipe, omitting ricotta filling. Instead, coarsely chop some cooked asparagus and mix into the mascarpone with some freshly grated Parmesan, salt, pepper, and 1 egg. Fill ravioli and cook as before.

ravioli di funghi e noci *(mushroom & walnut-stuffed ravioli)*
Prepare basic recipe, omitting the ricotta filling. Instead, combine some finely chopped cooked mushrooms with chopped toasted walnuts, mascarpone, salt, pepper, chopped fresh parsley, and 1 egg. Fill the ravioli.

ravioli di barbabietole *(ravioli with beets)*
Prepare basic recipe using 1/3 less of the ricotta. Purée or mash 1 cooked beet and mix with the ricotta to make a bright pink mixture. Flavor with a little ground cinnamon, salt, and pepper. Add 1 egg and fill ravioli.

ravioli di zucca *(pumpkin-stuffed ravioli)*
Prepare basic recipe, omitting ricotta filling. Instead purée cooked, peeled pumpkin or winter squash and mix with a few crumbled amaretto biscuits, some grated Parmesan, salt and pepper to taste, and 1 egg.

variations

tortellini in brodo
tortellini in broth

see base recipe page 104

tortellini al ragú alla bolognese *(tortellini with bolognese sauce)*
Prepare basic recipe for filled tortellini; omit broth. Cook the tortellini in salted water, drain, and dress with warm ragú alla bolognese (page 89) before dusting with freshly grated Parmesan to serve.

tortellini alla panna *(tortellini with cream)*
Prepare basic recipe for filled tortellini; omit broth. Cook the tortellini in salted water, drain, and dress with warmed heavy cream, lightly flavored with a dusting of freshly grated nutmeg. Dust with Parmesan and freshly ground black pepper.

tortellini di burro e salvia *(tortellini with butter & sage)*
Prepare basic recipe for filled tortellini; omit broth. Cook tortellini in salted water, drain, and dress with sage butter (page 125). Sprinkle with freshly grated Parmesan and serve.

tortellini di salmone *(tortellini with salmon)*
Omit broth and filling. Mix some poached salmon, a few spoonfuls of mascarpone cheese, 1 egg, salt, and pepper. Fill the tortellini. Cook in salted boiling water, drain, and dress with melted butter and a little grated lemon zest.

variations

rotolo di pasta alle barbabietole
pasta roll with beets

see base recipe page 106

rotolo di pasta alle noci *(pasta roll with walnuts)*
Instead of beet filling, mix the mascarpone cheese with chopped walnuts, freshly chopped parsley, and freshly grated Parmesan. Fill roll, cook, then serve with sage butter (page 125).

rotolo di pasta con peperoni e mozzarella *(pasta roll with peppers & mozzarella)*
Prepare basic recipe, but instead of beet filling, line sheet of pasta with slices of roasted red pepper (blotted dry) covered with very thin slices of mozzarella. Omit melted butter and poppy seeds and serve with a spoonful of pomodoro sauce (page 86) and a sprinkling of freshly grated Parmesan.

rotolo di pasta con ricotta e spinaci *(pasta roll with ricotta & spinach)*
Prepare basic recipe, but instead of beet filling, use spinach–ricotta filling (page 117). Instead of melted butter and poppy seeds, serve with melted butter and Parmesan, or pomodoro sauce (page 86).

primi piatti: gnocchi, risotti e pizze

first course: gnocchi, risotto & pizza

Comforting gnocchi, velvety risotto, polenta, and pizza make up the recipes in this chapter. These are recipes that could in many cases serve as an alternative primo or first course to a pasta dish.

gnocchi ai quattro formaggi
four-cheese gnocchi

see variations page 137

Making potato gnocchi is not the easiest thing to do, but the results are much more delicious than anything you can buy. Make sure the potatoes are as floury (starchy) as possible. Russet and Idaho potatoes have a high starch content, so they're good for gnocchi. The cooked gnocchi can be dressed with a wide variety of sauces, just like pasta. The following is a very rich cheesy dish.

2 lbs. floury potatoes, scrubbed
3 eggs, beaten
1/2 cup all-purpose flour, plus more for dusting
sea salt
1/4 lb. freshly grated Parmesan (preferably parmigiano reggiano)

generous 1/4 lb. fontina, thinly sliced
1/4 lb. Gorgonzola, cubed
1/4 lb. groviera, cubed or grated
1 1/4 cups light cream

Boil the potatoes until soft, drain, and peel quickly. Press through a potato ricer twice. Blend in the eggs and flour. Make a soft dough with your hands, then roll it into long rolls the thickness of your thumb on a floured board. Cut into half-inch lengths and form into gnocchi by gently pressing each one onto the floured surface with the tines of a fork to leave ridges in the dough. You will need about 12 gnocchi per person. Spread the gnocchi out on a large floured board until required.

Bring a large pot of salted water to a gentle boil, drop in the gnocchi in small batches, and cook until they float on the surface. Scoop out with a slotted spoon and arrange in a well-buttered ovenproof dish. Cover with all the cheeses, then pour cream on top. Bake in a preheated oven at 375°F for about 25 minutes, or until well browned. Serve at once.

Serves 6

gnocchi di semolino alla romana
roman-style semolina gnocchi

see variations page 138

This is the ultimate in comfort food, a delicately flavored dish of rounded gnocchi made out of cooked semolina, coated in butter and cheese, and baked until golden brown.

4 cups milk
1 cup semolina
2 egg yolks
1/4 lb. Parmesan, freshly grated

1/2 cup (1 stick) butter
pinch of ground nutmeg
sea salt and freshly ground black pepper

Bring the milk to a boil in a large saucepan. Reduce the heat to low, sprinkle in the semolina, and whisk constantly to prevent lumps forming. Continue until the mixture begins to thicken, then use a wooden spoon to stir constantly for about 10 minutes. You will know the mixture is thick enough when it begins to come away from the sides and bottom of the pan and forms a rounded, soft ball. Remove the pan from the heat. Stir in the egg yolks, half the Parmesan, and half the butter. Season to taste with nutmeg, salt, and pepper. Dampen a work surface lightly with cold water, then tip the semolina mixture onto it. Using a spatula dipped in cold water, spread flat to a thickness of about 1/2 inch. Using a 3-to-4-inch biscuit cutter, cut all the semolina into even-sized circles. Use some of the remaining butter to grease a shallow, ovenproof 10 x 12-inch dish. Arrange a layer of scraps from the cut-out circles on the bottom of dish. Cover with a little grated Parmesan and a few dots of butter. Cover with a layer of slightly overlapping semolina circles, and cover these with cheese and butter as before. Repeat until all ingredients have been used. Melt any remaining butter and trickle it over the top. Bake in a preheated 425°F oven for about 15 minutes before serving.

Serves 6

gnocchi di zucca con burro e salvia
pumpkin gnocchi with butter & sage

see variations page 139

These pumpkin gnocchi taste sweet and delicious and look gorgeous with their deep orange color. They are especially delectable when served with sage butter.

1 (1 1/2-lb.) fresh pumpkin (or winter squash)
1 cup all-purpose flour, plus more for rolling
2 eggs, beaten

2 oz. freshly grated Parmesan, plus more for serving
7 tbsp. butter
8–9 fresh sage leaves, lightly bruised

Peel the pumpkin or squash and remove seeds and all stringy parts. Cut into thick slices or chunks, and sprinkle with salt. Bake at 325°F on a sheet pan covered with parchment paper, until softened enough to mash with a fork, about 30–35 minutes. Remove from the oven and cool, then mash until completely smooth. (Do not use a food processor, as the purée will become too wet.) Working with small quantities at a time, gradually add the flour, eggs, and Parmesan. Mix gently with your hands, incorporating as much air as possible by not pressing down too hard. Sprinkle a clean surface with flour and roll the dough into a cylinder. With a sharp knife, cut into equal-sized sections, about an inch long. Lay the gnocchi on a floured surface, spaced apart, until required. Bring a large pot of salted water to a rolling boil, then lower the heat slightly to a gentle simmer. Melt the butter with the bruised sage over a low heat. Turn off the heat when butter is slightly browned. Drop the gnocchi gently into simmering water in batches of 6–8 at a time. Remove after they bob up to the surface, and transfer to the pan with sage butter. Spoon butter over them to coat. Continue with the next batch of gnocchi until they are all cooked. Transfer onto a warmed serving platter or individual plates. Sprinkle with freshly grated Parmesan and serve at once.

Serves 6

risotto alla parmigiana
parmesan risotto

see variations page 140

Cheese and butter risotto is the basic recipe from which all other risotto variations are created. Making risotto successfully is all about texture, so it is important to master a simple version like this one before moving on to more complicated recipes. Make sure you have the right kind of chalky rice for making risotto, and that you have a good, tasty stock. Risotto takes 20 minutes to make, from the moment the rice is added to the pot. For a risotto to be perfect, the rice needs to remain slightly chewy, with no trace of chalkiness.

6 tbsp. butter
1 medium onion, finely chopped
1 lb. risotto rice (Arborio, Vialone Nano, or
    Carnaroli)

4 cups (approximately) best-quality chicken or
    meat stock, or very strong-flavored
    vegetable stock, kept hot (pages 22–3)
6 tbsp. freshly grated Parmesan
sea salt and freshly ground black pepper

Fry the onion in half the butter for about 10 minutes over a very low heat, or until soft but not colored. Stir in rice and toast the grains thoroughly on all sides for about 5 minutes, over medium heat, so that they become opaque and thoroughly coated in butter. Move the pan off the heat for a few moments if the rice looks like it is browning. Add the first 3 ladlefuls of hot stock and stir. Then, stirring constantly, add the stock one ladle at a time, letting the rice absorb the liquid at its own pace. You will know when to add more stock when a clear wake through the grains opens up behind the spoon as you draw it through the cooking risotto. When the rice is almost completely soft and creamy, stir in the cheese and the rest of the butter. Taste and adjust the seasoning, then cover and rest for about 3 minutes, covered with a lid, before transferring to a platter to serve.

Serves 6

risotto alla sbirraglia
venetian chicken risotto

see variations page 141

This risotto with chicken is a typically Venetian risotto, wet and runny, but also very rich and filling. Make sure the chicken stock is very flavorsome to ensure that the finished risotto tastes properly rich. Although traditionally the risotto is served without any added color, you could stir a bit of parsley into the finished dish if you feel it needs a touch of green.

1/2 cup (1 stick) butter
1/2 onion, chopped finely
1 lb. skinless chicken, diced
scant 1/2 cup dry white wine
2 cups risotto rice (Vialone Nano, Vialone
    Gigante, or Arborio)

4 cups (approximately) rich chicken stock
    (page 23)
3 oz. Parmesan, freshly grated
sea salt and freshly ground black pepper

Melt half the butter in a deep saucepan on a low heat. Add the onion and fry until just pale golden, then add diced chicken. Cook chicken very gently until lightly browned, then pour in the wine, raise heat, and cook quickly for about 2 minutes to allow the alcohol to burn off. Now add the rice. Stir thoroughly, lower the heat, then add the stock gradually, one ladleful at a time, stirring constantly until it is absorbed. Continue until the rice is tender, and most or all of the stock has been used. Stir in the remaining butter and half the cheese. Remove from the heat and cover. Rest for about 3 minutes, transfer to a warmed platter, sprinkle with remaining cheese, and serve.

Serves 6

risotto con la salsiccia
sausage risotto

see variations page 142

This very filling, meaty risotto uses delicious Italian sausages and is a great favorite as a rustic dish.

4 large Italian sausages, casings removed, crumbled
1 onion, peeled and chopped
1–2 cloves garlic, peeled and chopped
1 small sprig fresh rosemary, chopped
4–5 tbsp. light olive oil

1 1/4 cups dry white wine
2 cups risotto rice such as Arborio
4 2/3 cups hot chicken or vegetable stock (page 23)
sea salt and freshly ground black pepper
freshly grated Parmesan, to serve (optional)

Put crumbled sausages, onion, garlic, and rosemary into a large heavy-bottomed saucepan with olive oil. Fry gently until onion is cooked. Add the white wine and stir. Wait for the alcohol fumes to boil off, then add the rice and begin the cooking process, adding a little hot stock at a time and waiting for the rice to absorb it, stirring thoroughly each time you add more liquid. Continue in this way until rice is tender and all the grains are plump and fluffy. Season to taste with salt and pepper. Remove from heat, stir, and cover. Let stand for about 3 minutes before transferring to a platter and serving. Offer Parmesan separately, if desired.

Serves 6

polenta ai funghi
polenta with mushrooms

see variations page 143

Polenta is a staple of the Northern Italian diet. You can buy a quick-cook version, which you mix up in just 5 minutes. Using traditional polenta, you need to stir constantly for about 50 minutes, but the end result is very different from the quick-cook kind. Because it is such a time-consuming operation, it's easier to make a large batch, serve it fresh the first time, and then let it set before slicing to be fried or grilled in subsequent days.

6 cups cold water
large pinch sea salt
1 1/3 cups ground cornmeal (polenta)
1 lb. fresh porcini, oyster, or other mushrooms
    of your choice, cleaned, trimmed, washed

4–5 tbsp. olive oil
3–4 cloves garlic, finely chopped
sea salt and freshly ground black pepper
1 large pinch finely chopped fresh rosemary

To make polenta, pour cold water into a wide, heavy-bottomed, preferably copper pan and place over high heat. Bring to a boil. Trickle the polenta into boiling water in a fine rain with one hand, and whisk constantly with the other. When all the polenta has been whisked into water, reduce heat to medium-low and begin to stir with a strong, long-handled wooden spoon until polenta comes away from the sides of pan. This will take 40–50 minutes. Turn the polenta out onto a wooden board and smooth it into a mound using 2 spatulas or wooden spoons. Let it stand for about 5 minutes. While the polenta stands, slice mushrooms finely. Heat oil and garlic together in a large saucepan on medium heat for about 1 minute, then add mushrooms. Stir, season, and cover. Allow mushrooms to cook through, stirring occasionally. When mushrooms are cooked, stir in rosemary. Cover and let stand for another 2 minutes before serving, piping hot, with slabs of polenta.

Serves 6

pizza marinara
marinara pizza

see variations page 144

This is the recipe for one of the first pizzas, long before the introduction of the myriad of other ingredients that are now common on pizzas the world over. Interestingly, it does not include mozzarella. Though its name translates as "sailor's pizza," it does not contain any seafood—it was made in Naples for sailors when they returned from the sea.

for the pizza dough
1 1/4 oz. fresh yeast
1 scant cup warm water
pinch sugar
1/4 tsp. sea salt
4 cups white bread flour
2–3 tsp. olive oil

for the topping
3/4 cup canned tomatoes, puréed
4 cloves garlic, finely chopped
1 heaped tsp. dried oregano
12 tbsp. olive oil
about 16 leaves fresh basil
salt and freshly ground black pepper
extra olive oil for greasing

Mix yeast and water with sugar and salt, then add about 2 tablespoons flour. Put the yeast mixture in a lightly floured bowl and place it somewhere warm to rise for about 30 minutes. Put the rest of the flour on a work surface. Knead the yeast mixture thoroughly, then knead it into the rest of the flour, adding a little more water as required. Add half the oil and knead energetically for about 10 minutes. Transfer the mixture to a large floured bowl, cover with plastic wrap, lightly oiled on the underside to prevent the rising dough from sticking to it, and return to the warm place to rise again for about 1 hour or until doubled in size.

Preheat the oven to 425°F. Divide the dough into 6 equal parts. Roll each part out thinly and arrange on oiled baking sheets. When spreading out the dough, dip your fingers in cold water in order to bring as much moisture as possible into the dough itself as it bakes. Cover

thinly with puréed canned tomatoes, leaving a border of about 1 1/2 inches around the edges. Sprinkle with garlic, oregano, the remaining olive oil, basil, and a little salt and pepper. Bake until the border is crisp and the pizza dough is dry on the bottom, and serve warm.

Serves 6

calzone
folded pizza

see variations page 145

A calzone, meaning a "pair of trousers," is made of pizza dough with a variety of fillings inside, folded in half and sealed before baking. Calzoni can be eaten as they are, or served with a bowl of pomodoro all'aglio (page 109) on the side. Sometimes, the filled and folded calzoni are deep-fried instead of baked. This recipe starts with 1 of the 6 circles of pizza dough from the recipe on page 134, and is easily expanded to serve more people. If you want to make 6 large calzoni, double the quantity of basic dough.

1 circle basic pizza dough (page 134)
2 tbsp. fresh ricotta
3 slices salami, chopped coarsely
2 sun-dried tomatoes in olive oil, drained and
    chopped

1 tsp. chopped fresh flat-leaf parsley
extra-virgin olive oil for greasing and brushing
sea salt and freshly ground black pepper

Preheat the oven to 400°F. Place the circle of pizza dough on an oiled baking sheet. Spread ricotta onto half the circle, keeping to the center so you can fold it in half and seal it easily. Sprinkle salami, sun-dried tomato, and parsley on top of the ricotta. Drizzle with a little olive oil and season lightly with salt and pepper. Fold the calzone in half and seal the edge well with the back of a fork. Bake for about 15 minutes, then serve with a bowl of tomato sauce on the side.

Makes 1

gnocchi ai quattro formaggi
four-cheese gnocchi

see base recipe page 121

gnocchi al pomodoro e basilico *(gnocchi with basil)*
Prepare and cook gnocchi. Instead of four cheeses and cream, dress hot gnocchi with a handful of freshly picked basil leaves, some cubed fresh tomatoes, and a little melted butter. Mix very gently, add a little salt and pepper and a handful of freshly grated Parmesan, and serve.

gnocchi al prezzemolo con funghi e fontina *(gnocchi with mushrooms & fontina)*
Before shaping and cooking gnocchi, mix a little finely chopped fresh parsley into dough. Instead of four cheeses and cream, gently toss hot gnocchi with some warm sautéed mushrooms, a little warmed heavy cream, and some grated fontina cheese.

gnocchi al ragú *(gnocchi with ragú)*
Prepare and cook gnocchi. Instead of four cheeses and cream, gently toss hot gnocchi with ragú (page 89).

gnocchi al pomodoro *(gnocchi with tomato sauce)*
Prepare and cook gnocchi. Instead of four cheeses and cream, gently toss hot gnocchi with pomodoro sauce (page 86).

gnocchi con gorgonzola & noci *(gnocchi with gorgonzola & walnuts)*
Prepare and cook gnocchi. Instead of four cheeses and cream, gently toss hot gnocchi with soft, cubed Gorgonzola and a handful of toasted, chopped walnuts.

variations

gnocchi di semolino alla romana
roman-style semolina gnocchi

see base recipe page 122

gnocchi di semolino allo zafferano *(gnocchi with semolina & saffron)*
Prepare basic recipe, but add a little saffron to the semolina mixture for a
lightly spiced and deep golden yellow gnocchi.

gnocchi di semolino con salmone affumicato *(semolina gnocchi with
smoked salmon)*
Prepare basic recipe. Scatter a little chopped smoked salmon among the
layers of gnocchi before baking.

gnocchi di semolino con gorgonzola *(semolina gnocchi & gorgonzola)*
Prepare basic recipe. Add a few cubes of Gorgonzola among the layers of
gnocchi before baking.

gnocchi di semolino con burro e salvia *(semolina gnocchi with sage butter)*
Prepare basic recipe. Instead of layering the gnocchi with cubes of butter, melt
the remaining 4 tablespoons of butter with a few fresh sage leaves and drizzle
over the gnocchi. Add Parmesan and bake as normal.

gnocchi di semolino con mozzarella e pomodorini *(semolina gnocchi with
mozzarella & cherry tomatoes)*
Prepare basic recipe. Add some halved cherry tomatoes and cubes of
mozzarella among the layers of gnocchi before baking.

variations

gnocchi di zucca con burro e salvia
pumpkin gnocchi with butter & sage

see base recipe page 125

gnocchi di zucca con pinoli e parmigiano *(pumpkin gnocchi with pine nuts & parmesan)*
Prepare basic recipe, omitting the sage butter. Dress the hot gnocchi with melted butter, toasted pine nuts, and freshly grated Parmesan.

gnocchi di zucca al gorgonzola *(pumpkin gnocchi with butter & gorgonzola)*
Prepare basic recipe, omitting the sage butter. In a double boiler, melt some Gorgonzola in enough cream or milk to cover until smooth. Spoon the sauce over the hot gnocchi and sprinkle with just a little freshly grated Parmesan.

gnocchi di zucca al pomodoro con panna *(pumpkin gnocchi with cherry tomatoes & cream)*
Prepare basic recipe, omitting the sage butter. Dress the hot gnocchi with warmed heavy cream and coarsely chopped cherry tomatoes. Add some freshly grated Parmesan and a handful of fresh basil leaves to serve.

gnocchi di zucca al pomodoro e mascarpone *(pumpkin gnocchi with cherry tomatoes & mascarpone)*
Prepare basic recipe, omitting the sage butter. Dress the hot gnocchi with pomodoro con mascarpone (page 109). Add some freshly grated Parmesan and a handful of fresh basil leaves to serve.

variations

risotto alla parmigiana
parmesan risotto

see base recipe page 126

risotto al prezzemolo *(parsley risotto)*
Prepare basic recipe, adding a large handful of fresh flat-leaf parsley, finely chopped, at the very end of the cooking time.

risotto al vino rosso *(red wine risotto)*
Prepare basic recipe, substituting half the stock for a really good red wine.

risotto al gorgonzola *(risotto with gorgonzola)*
Prepare basic recipe, adding about 5 ounces cubed Gorgonzola to melt in the risotto just before covering and resting. Give the risotto one final stir just before serving. Offer grated Parmesan separately at the table.

risotto con spinaci e noci *(risotto with spinach & walnuts)*
Prepare basic recipe, but about halfway through the cooking process, add a couple of handfuls of finely chopped fresh spinach to the rice. Just before resting, stir in a handful of roughly chopped walnuts.

risotto ai funghi *(mushroom risotto)*
Prepare basic recipe, but add about 1/2 pound sliced mushrooms with the onion at the start, then add the rice and continue as normal.

risotto alla sbirraglia
venetian chicken risotto

see base recipe page 128

risotto ai fegatini *(risotto with liver)*
Prepare the basic recipe, omitting the chicken. Instead, cook 1 cup cleaned, roughly chopped chicken livers in butter until just browned. Add a spoonful of brandy and flame the livers, then remove from the heat. Stir the livers into the risotto about 5 minutes before risotto is cooked through.

risotto di pancetta e pollo *(risotto with pancetta)*
Prepare basic recipe, adding some chopped smoked pancetta to the onion and chicken at the beginning of the cooking process.

risotto all'anatra *(risotto with duck)*
Prepare basic recipe, replacing the chicken with finely chopped, skinless duck. Make sure it is well cooked and tender before adding rice.

risotto al coniglio *(risotto with rabbit)*
Replace chicken with finely chopped, skinless rabbit. Double the amount of onion and add 1 1/2 teaspoons finely chopped fresh sage before cooking rice.

risotto al pollo, zucca e mandorle *(risotto with chicken, squash & almonds)*
Add about 1 cup diced butternut squash to the chicken at the beginning of the cooking process. Make sure it is well softened before adding the rice. At the end, just before resting the risotto, stir in 1/2 cup toasted slivered almonds.

variations

risotto con la salsiccia
sausage risotto

see base recipe page 131

risotto al ragú alla bolognese *(risotto with bolognese sauce)*
Omit sausages. Before adding wine, let rice toast, not brown, with onion. Stir in some ragú alla bolognese (page 89) before adding stock. Add a couple of tablespoons of freshly grated Parmesan to the risotto just before resting.

risotto con funghi e salsiccia *(mushroom risotto)*
Add a small handful of dried porcini mushrooms (soaked in warm water until soft, then drained and chopped) to sausages at start of cooking process.

risotto all'agnello *(lamb risotto)*
Replace sausages with lamb removed from 8 small chops and cubed.

risotto di caccia *(venison risotto)*
To give the risotto a rich, gamey flavor, replace sausages with chopped, tender venison or other game meat.

risotto con pomodoro e pancetta *(tomato & pancetta risotto)*
Prepare basic recipe, replacing the sausages with 8 chopped strips of smoked pancetta and 1 large tablespoon concentrated tomato paste, diluted in a little warm water. Garnish the finished risotto with a handful of chopped fresh mushrooms and a couple of crisply cooked and crumbled pancetta strips.

polenta ai funghi
polenta with mushroom

see base recipe page 132

polenta con salsicce *(polenta with sausage)*
Prepare polenta, but omit mushrooms. Fry 12 Italian sausages gently with
1 chopped onion and a little olive oil. Add 2 (14-ounce) cans of chopped
tomatoes, a sprig of rosemary, and 1 bay leaf. Cover and simmer gently for
about 30 minutes, stirring occasionally. Serve on top of hot polenta slices.

polenta con spezzatino di manzo *(polenta with beef stew)*
Prepare polenta, but omit mushrooms. Serve a slice of polenta, covered with
a ladleful of beef stew (page 205), for each person.

polenta con pesce lesso *(polenta with poached fish)*
Prepare polenta, but omit mushrooms. Poach 6 chunky fillets of haddock or
cod in enough milk to cover, with a bay leaf, salt, and pepper. When the fish
is cooked through, remove it and allow the milk to reduce, stirring until
slightly thickened. Serve each slice of polenta with a fillet and some milk.

polenta con gorgonzola *(polenta with gorgonzola)*
Prepare polenta, but omit mushrooms. Slice the set polenta and grill on both
sides until browned. Cover each slice with Gorgonzola and return to grill to
melt cheese before serving.

variations

pizza marinara
pizza marinara

see base recipe page 134

pizza margherita *(pizza margherita)*
Omit garlic and oregano and add mozzarella slices.

pizza ai funghi *(mushroom pizza)*
Prepare basic pizza, omitting garlic, oregano, and basil, and adding some
cooked mushrooms and sliced mozzarella.

pizza con la rucola *(arugula pizza)*
Omit garlic and oregano and add mozzarella slices. When the pizza is
cooked, add 2 handfuls of fresh arugula leaves before serving.

pizza al prosciutto di Parma *(pizza with parma ham)*
Prepare basic recipe, omitting garlic and oregano and adding mozzarella
slices. Bake the pizza for half the required time. Remove from the oven, lay
4 paper-thin slices of Parma ham over the pizza, drizzle again with olive oil,
and return to the oven to finish baking.

pizza al salame *(pizza with salami)*
Prepare basic recipe, omitting garlic and basil and adding mozzarella slices,
then slices of your favorite salami.

calzone
folded pizza

see base recipe page 136

calzone al ragú *(folded pizza with ragú)*
Instead of salami filling, use some of the ragú (page 89) with a few slices of mozzarella and a little freshly grated Parmesan.

calzone di verdure *(folded vegetable pizza)*
Instead of salami filling, use cooked vegetables such as zucchini, eggplant, peppers, and tomatoes with a few cubes of mozzarella.

calzone di bufala *(folded mozzarella pizza)*
Instead of salami filling, fill the calzone with cubes of buffalo mozzarella, a drizzle of olive oil, a sprinkling of dried oregano, and salt and pepper.

calzone con prosciutto e piselli *(folded pizza with prosciutto & peas)*
Instead of salami filling, fill the calzone with peas cooked in olive oil, chopped onions, and cubes of ham.

calzone con mortadella *(folded pizza with Italian sausage)*
Instead of salami filling, fill the calzone with chopped mortadella, ricotta, salt, pepper, and a sprinkling of chopped fresh flat-leaf parsley.

verdure
vegetables

Seasonal vegetables are one of the most glorious

things about Italian food. Here's a variety of recipes

that show how to prepare them imaginatively,

turning them not only into perfect side dishes, but

also into complete dishes on their own.

cianfotta
italian vegetable stew

see variations page 167

The texture of this dish is very soft and squashy, almost like a chutney. This is an Italian version of French ratatouille. It is very important to use very sweet peppers and to keep everything moist during the cooking process. It's fabulous, either hot or cold, with chicken or fish, on its own as part of an antipasto, or as a light main course.

1 lb. yellow or red sweet peppers
1 lb. unpeeled eggplant
4 tbsp. extra-virgin olive oil
generous 1/2 lb. small onions, halved

generous 1/2 lb. small tomatoes, halved
3/4–1 cup dry white wine
sea salt and freshly ground black pepper

Remove the seeds and inner membranes from the peppers, then cut into even-sized chunks. Cut the eggplant into even-sized cubes. Put the cubes into a colander and sprinkle with salt. Cover with a plate, weigh the plate down with something heavy like a can of tomatoes, and let drain over sink or large bowl for about 1 hour. Rinse and dry the cubes. In a large pot, heat the oil, then add the onions. Cook the onions until just soft, then add eggplant, peppers, and tomatoes. Sprinkle with wine and add salt and pepper to taste. Cover and simmer gently for about 1 hour, keeping the heat low and stirring frequently. Serve hot or cold.

Serves 6

melanzane alla parmigiana
baked eggplant with tomato & parmesan

see variations page 168

Popularly known as eggplant parmigiana, the traditional recipe for this dish from the region of Campania, in southern Italy, calls for the eggplant to be fried in oil before being used in this dish. In this much lighter version, the eggplant is brushed with oil and broiled or grilled until softened.

3 long (Japanese) eggplant, unpeeled, cut into
   1/4-inch-thick rounds
sea salt
6 tbsp. extra-virgin olive oil
1 1/2 cups pomodoro sauce (page 86)

10 oz. fresh mozzarella, sliced
6 oz. freshly grated Parmesan
about 15 fresh basil leaves, torn
freshly ground black pepper

Sprinkle eggplant slices with salt and lay them in a wide colander. Put a plate on top, and a weight on the plate. Leave colander in the sink for 1 hour to let the bitter juices drain away. You may need to do this in batches. Rinse and pat the slices dry, then brush lightly with oil. Use the remaining oil to lightly grease a large ovenproof dish. Turn on the oven broiler. Lay oiled eggplant slices on a broiler pan and place pan under the broiler. (You may also grill eggplant slices, if desired.) Broil them until soft and lightly browned, turning them several times. Spread a layer of tomato sauce over the bottom of the ovenproof dish. Cover with a layer of grilled eggplant slices, a layer of mozzarella, a layer of tomato sauce, a sprinkling of Parmesan, and a few torn basil leaves. Repeat until the ingredients are all used. Finish with a thick layer of tomato sauce, a sprinkling of Parmesan, and a little basil. You can make this ahead to this stage, then bake when required. Bake in a preheated 375°F oven for about 20 minutes, then remove and allow to stand for about 5 minutes before slicing and serving.

Serves 6

funghi al forno
baked mushrooms

see variations page 169

Choose the biggest mushrooms you can find for these baked stuffed mushrooms. Fall in Italy heralds the start of the porcini season and you can find huge fresh ones for sale at virtually every street vegetable stall, but any tasty mushroom with a good dense texture will work very well. You can, of course, vary the type of cheese according to your own preferences.

6 very large mushrooms
6 tbsp. ricotta
4 tbsp. very soft Gorgonzola
4 tbsp. freshly grated Parmesan
4 tbsp. soft white bread crumbs

2 tbsp. chopped fresh flat-leaf parsley
5 tbsp. extra-virgin olive oil
sea salt and freshly ground black pepper

Preheat the oven to 350°F. Wipe the mushrooms clean and remove their stems. Chop the stems up very small and put into a bowl. Add ricotta, Gorgonzola, half the Parmesan, bread crumbs, and parsley. Season with salt and pepper. Use the resulting mixture to fill the mushrooms generously. With 1 tablespoon olive oil, brush an ovenproof dish large enough for all the mushrooms to sit in flat. Place the filled mushrooms in the dish. Sprinkle the remaining Parmesan on top of the mushrooms. Drizzle the remaining oil around and over the mushrooms. Bake for about 25 minutes, or until soft and golden brown on top. Serve at once.

Serves 6

piselli con la pancetta
peas with pancetta

see variations page 170

This classic pea with pancetta dish makes a delicious side dish. It is also a wonderful filling for an omelet or mixed with freshly cooked pasta and a little cream.

7 oz. pancetta, chopped
2 onions, chopped
4 tbsp. olive oil

1 lb. frozen or fresh peas
sea salt and freshly ground black pepper

Fry pancetta, onions, and oil together until the pancetta is lightly browned and crisp. Add the peas and stir together thoroughly. Keep moist as you braise the peas until tender, adding water when they appear to be drying out. Season to taste with salt and pepper and serve.

Serves 6

terrina di peperoni e mozzarella
french bean, pepper & mozzarella terrine

see variations page 171

This pretty pepper and mozzarella terrine is cooked in just over half an hour. Make sure that there are no gaps between the layers, as this will prevent the terrine from being turned out successfully. Also, use a really sharp knife to slice the finished terrine neatly.

3 leeks, trimmed
2 red peppers
2 yellow peppers
10 oz. green beans, topped and tailed
14 oz. buffalo mozzarella, cubed

4 tbsp. extra-virgin olive oil
5 eggs, beaten
sea salt and freshly ground black pepper
2 tbsp. freshly grated Parmesan

Cut the leeks in half lengthwise. Strip off larger leaves to blanch for 1 minute in boiling salted water, then drop into a bowl of cold water. Slice rest of leeks thinly and set aside. Roast peppers in the oven, on the barbecue, or under broiler until blackened, then cool and peel, removing all seeds and membranes. Cut peppers into neat strips. Boil green beans in salted water for about 8 minutes, then drain and refresh in cold water. In a skillet, heat oil, add raw sliced leeks and green beans, and sauté gently for about 5 minutes. Line a loaf pan with waxed paper and heat oven to 350°F. Season eggs with salt and pepper, then add Parmesan. Line pan with the wide, long leek leaves, allowing them to fall out over the sides. Arrange a layer of pepper stips on bottom of terrine, cover with beaten egg and mozzarella cubes, then add a layer of green beans and leeks; then more egg and mozzarella, more pepper — until pan is full and ingredients have been used up. Wrap leek leaves back over the top of the filled terrine and press down gently. Cover loosely with foil, and bake in preheated oven for 20 minutes. After 20 minutes, uncover and finish baking for about 15 minutes. Cool for at least 20 minutes before slicing. Serve at room temperature, with a green salad.

Serves 6

rambasici
stuffed cabbage leaves

see variations page 172

This recipe for stuffed cabbage leaves from Friuli–Venezia Giulia has a dialect name that means "escaped birds," as the swollen leaves are supposed to look like little birds hiding from hunters' guns. You'll need only the green leaves, some of which will be large enough to cut in half once you have blanched them. This makes a satisfying winter dish, and only needs boiled potatoes and good red wine to make it into a delicious supper.

12 large leaves Savoy cabbage
sea salt and freshly ground black pepper
10 oz. lean ground pork
10 oz. lean ground beef
3 tbsp. chopped fresh flat-leaf parsley
2 cloves garlic, finely chopped
2 hard-boiled eggs, finely chopped
2 slices whole-wheat bread cut into small cubes

2–3 slices salami, cut into small squares
6 tbsp. vegetable oil or 4 tbsp. butter
1 large onion, sliced
1 1/4 cups warm meat stock (page 22)
1 heaping tbsp. dry bread crumbs
1 heaping tbsp. freshly grated Parmesan
2 tbsp. olive oil

Blanch cabbage leaves for 1 minute in boiling salted water, drain carefully, and arrange flat on a work surface, ready to fill. Mix together meats, parsley, garlic, hard-boiled eggs, bread, and salami. Divide this mixture evenly between each cabbage leaf. Roll up leaves, close rolls with 2 toothpicks, and set aside. You should have about 12 rambasici. Heat oil or butter in a wide pan and fry onion until soft. Add rambasici to pan in a single layer. Cover with half the stock, reduce to a low simmer, and cook for about 15 minutes, then add remaining stock and cook for a further 15 minutes. In a separate small pan, fry bread crumbs and Parmesan in the olive oil until crisp. Arrange rambasici on a warmed platter, pour remaining cooking juices around them, sprinkle with fried bread crumbs and Parmesan, and serve at once.

Serves 6

torta pasqualina
easter pie

see variations page 173

The custom of serving a savory cake or pie is common in various parts of Italy, especially in regions such as Liguria and Le Marche, as well as in parts of the south. This recipe is for the traditional Easter savory cake, served traditionally on Easter Monday.

2 3/4 cups all-purpose flour, plus extra
   for dusting
sea salt
generous 1/2 cup warm water
4 tbsp. extra-virgin olive oil
1 large onion, chopped
6 artichokes preserved in oil

14 oz. fresh spinach leaves, washed
large handful of fresh flat-leaf parsley, chopped
1 lb. ricotta
2 oz. Parmesan, freshly grated
6 eggs
freshly ground black pepper

To make the pastry, mix the flour and a pinch of salt in a bowl. Add the water and half the oil and mix to a smooth dough. Knead for 5 minutes on a floured surface, until soft and stretchy. Cover with plastic wrap and set aside for 15 minutes. To make the filling, heat the remaining oil in a large pan over medium heat. Fry the onion for 8 minutes, stirring occasionally. Stir in the artichokes and toss for a few minutes. Pile spinach on top, cover the pan, and wilt over a gentle heat. Set aside to cool slightly. Put the filling mixture in a food processor with the parsley, cheeses, and 3 eggs. Season well with salt and pepper, pulse, and set aside. Preheat the oven to 425°F. Roll out two-thirds of the pastry on a floured surface to a large circle. Use to line base and sides of a deep, 11-inch, loose-bottomed cake pan. Spoon in the filling. Smooth, make 2 deep indents, and crack in 2 eggs. Roll out remaining pastry to a circle and lay on top. Twist edges to seal. Beat remaining egg, brush over pastry, and sprinkle with sea salt. Bake for 30–35 minutes, until golden. Slice and serve.

Serves 6

mosaico di verdura

vegetable mosaic

see variations page 174

Vegetable mosaic is a wonderful, hot vegetable dish that is perfect for a light supper or a vegetarian lunchtime treat if you omit the ham. Serve with the tomato sauce and plenty of crusty bread.

9 oz. small white potatoes, peeled
1/4 lb. carrots, scraped
1/4 lb. green beans, topped and tailed
1/4 lb. asparagus spears
1/2 lb. frozen, fresh, or canned peas
1/2 onion, very finely chopped
2 heaping tbsp. freshly grated Parmesan
2 oz. Parma ham, finely chopped (optional)
2 tbsp. chopped fresh flat-leaf parsley
sea salt and freshly ground black pepper
1 cup light cream

4 egg yolks
butter for greasing
for the sauce
1/2 onion, very finely chopped
2 tbsp. butter
1 tbsp. tomato paste, diluted in 2 tbsp. warm water
1 (14-oz.) can chopped tomatoes, drained
sea salt and freshly ground black pepper
3 tbsp. chopped fresh flat-leaf parsley

Boil or steam the potatoes and carrots separately until tender. Drain, cool, then cut into small cubes. Boil or steam the beans, asparagus, and peas separately, then drain and cut into similar-sized pieces. Preheat the oven to 350°F. Put the vegetables in a bowl. Add the onion and stir in carefully. Add the Parmesan, ham (if using), and parsley. Mix together gently, then season to taste with salt and pepper. In a separate bowl, mix the cream and egg yolks together, then stir gently into vegetables.

Butter a 1-quart ring mold, then pour in vegetable mixture. Place mold in a baking pan, and add water to come two-thirds up the sides of mold. Bake for about 30 minutes, or until set.

Meanwhile, make the sauce. Fry the onion in butter until transparent. Add the diluted tomato paste and canned tomatoes, stir, season, and cover. Simmer gently for about 25 minutes, stirring occasionally. Remove from the heat, stir in the parsley, and keep warm until required. Loosen edges of mosaic with a knife or spatula and turn out onto a serving dish. Drizzle some sauce over it and serve immediately, with sauce offered separately.

Serves 6

torta di zucchini
zucchini cake

see variations page 175

This savory zucchini cake is a delicious starter or a dish substantial enough for a light lunch with a salad. You could also use artichokes, fennel, or a combination of potatoes and onions to make this lovely specialty from Liguria, which is reminiscent of the eggplant recipe on page 148.

12 medium-sized zucchini, topped and tailed
2 small onions
6 tbsp. butter
1/3 cup extra-virgin olive oil
2 tbsp. chopped fresh flat-leaf parsley
1 tsp. fresh marjoram leaves

sea salt and freshly ground black pepper
1/3 cup light cream, sour cream, or whole milk
6 eggs, beaten
1/2 cup freshly grated Parmesan
6 tbsp. Italian dry bread crumbs (Pangrattato preferred)

Preheat oven to 375°F. Slice the zucchini into rounds or cubes and place in a colander to drain for half an hour or so. Rinse and dry. Meanwhile, slice the onions finely and fry gently without browning in butter and half the oil. Use half the remaining oil to grease a ring mold or ovenproof dish. Add the sliced zucchini to the onions and continue to cook gently, stirring frequently. When zucchini are soft and onions are cooked, set aside to cool, then add the parsley, marjoram, salt, and pepper. In a separate bowl, beat the cream, sour cream, or milk with eggs and Parmesan, then add seasoning to taste. When the zucchini are cool, stir into the egg mixture. Sprinkle oiled mold or dish thoroughly with half the bread crumbs, making sure they stick to the sides and bottom thickly. Pour or spoon zucchini and egg mixture into the dish and bang it down lightly to allow it to settle. Sprinkle with remaining bread crumbs and drizzle with remaining oil. Bake for about 30 minutes, until firm. Remove from the oven and let cool slightly before turning out onto a serving dish. It can be enjoyed hot or cold.

Serves 6

frittata di zucchine
zucchini omelet

see variations page 176

When making a frittata, the ratio of vegetable to egg varies enormously, depending upon the vegetable you are using. The basic rule of thumb is that there has to be enough egg to hold the whole thing together, but there must be enough vegetable to form the main part of the finished frittata. It's best to use about 2/3 vegetable and 1/3 eggs. Be very careful not to add too much cheese, as it will make the frittata stick and thus make it impossible to turn successfully. The amount of time it takes to cook the frittata will depend on how thick it is, and what kind and size of pan you choose.

8 small zucchini, sliced into thin discs
2 onions, thinly sliced
6 tbsp. olive oil

sea salt and freshly ground black pepper
6 eggs, beaten
2 oz. Parmesan, freshly grated

Put the sliced zucchini and onions into a pan with half the oil, and fry until the onion is softened. Add a little water, salt, and pepper, and continue to cook until the zucchini are softened. You can add the hot cooked zucchini directly into the beaten eggs or wait until they cool before adding. Once the zucchini are mixed with the eggs, add the Parmesan, salt, and pepper. Heat the remaining oil in a wide, shallow pan over medium heat. When very hot, but before it smokes, pour in the egg mixture. Shake the pan to flatten and even out the mixture, pulling liquid egg into the center as you work. Cook until the underside is browned and firm. Turn the frittata over by covering the pan with a lid or plate and inverting the pan. Put the pan down on the heat, right-side up, and carefully slide the frittata (uncooked side down) back into the hot pan. Then cook again, for a shorter time, until golden brown and firm on the underside. Slide the frittata onto a clean, flat platter and serve hot or cold.

Serves 4–6

verdure alla griglia
grilled vegetables

see variations page 177

Lots of different fresh vegetables, carefully grilled and dressed with olive oil, make a delicious and very light main dish that can be turned into a filling meal by adding a few simple extras. You can, of course, leave out any of the following vegetables or use others too.

3 zucchini, sliced thinly lengthwise
4 red peppers, sliced lengthwise and seeded
1 large eggplant, sliced lengthwise (sprinkled
    with salt, left to stand in a colander under
    a weighted plate for an hour, rinsed,
    and dried)
1 large red onion, sliced across center into
    8 flat, thick slices (keep root stub intact
    so onion slices remain whole)

4 large, beefsteak tomatoes, sliced very thick
2 bulbs fennel, sliced very thick
6 tbsp. extra-virgin olive oil, plus more for
    serving
2 tbsp. chopped fresh flat-leaf parsley
sea salt and freshly ground black pepper

Heat the grill to medium. Grill each vegetable separately, brushed with olive oil, until just tender. As soon as they are cooked, arrange them in a shallow, warmed wide bowl or platter and sprinkle with chopped parsley, drizzle with olive oil, and season with salt and pepper, with the different vegetables overlapping each other. Serve at room temperature.

Serves 6

variations

cianfotta
vegetable stew

see base recipe page 147

cianfotta di peperoni e patate *(vegetable stew with peppers & potato)*
Prepare basic recipe, doubling amount of peppers, omitting eggplant, and adding
3 cubed, peeled potatoes. Sprinkle finished dish with a little white wine vinegar.

cianfotta con funghi *(vegetable stew with mushrooms)*
Prepare basic recipe, replacing eggplant with about 12 medium mushrooms, halved.

cianfotta con peperoncino *(hot pepper vegetable stew)*
Prepare basic recipe, adding 2 cloves garlic, chopped, and 1 dried red chile pepper,
chopped, to onions.

cianfotta con carciofi *(vegetable stew with artichoke hearts)*
Prepare basic recipe, replacing eggplant with 6 raw artichoke hearts.

cianfotta con la mozzarella *(vegetable stew with mozzarella)*
Prepare basic recipe, then transfer to an ovenproof dish, and dot with cubes of
2 balls of mozzarella. Slide under a hot broiler and allow the cheese to just melt
before serving.

variations

melanzane alla parmigiana
baked eggplant with tomato & parmesan

see base recipe page 148

parmigiana di zucchini *(baked zucchini with tomato & parmesan)*
Prepare basic recipe, substituting 6 large zucchini for the eggplant.

parmigiana di carciofi *(baked artichoke with tomato & parmesan)*
Prepare basic recipe, replacing eggplant with 20 artichoke bottoms. Boil
them in salted water until just tender. Drain and layer in dish in the same
way as the eggplant slices.

parmigiana di patate *(baked potatoes with tomato & parmesan)*
Prepare basic recipe, replacing the eggplant with peeled, thinly sliced,
parboiled potatoes.

parmigiana d'asparagi *(baked asparagus with tomato & parmesan)*
Prepare basic recipe, replacing the eggplant with large, plump asparagus,
either poached gently in salted water until tender, or oiled and grilled before
layering in dish.

parmigiana senza mozzarella *(baked eggplant with tomato & parmesan
without mozzarella)*
Prepare basic recipe, omitting all mozzarella and using plenty of freshly
grated Parmesan between the layers.

variations

funghi al forno

baked mushrooms

see base recipe page 151

funghi al forno con scamorza *(baked mushrooms with smoked cheese)*
Prepare basic recipe, replacing ricotta with grated smoked scamorza (air-dried, smoked mozzarella).

funghi a forno al pomodoro *(baked mushrooms with tomato sauce)*
Prepare basic recipe, but finish by topping each mushroom with a spoonful of pomodoro sauce (page 86) before finally sprinkling with Parmesan.

funghi a forno ai pinoli *(baked mushrooms with pine nuts)*
Prepare basic recipe, adding a handful of lightly toasted pine nuts to the filling.

funghi a forno con le noci *(baked mushrooms with walnuts)*
Prepare basic recipe, adding a handful of finely chopped walnuts to the filling.

funghi al forno con la pancetta *(pancetta-filled baked mushrooms)*
Prepare basic recipe, adding a handful of crisply fried pancetta cubes to the filling.

variations

piselli con la pancetta
peas with pancetta

see base recipe page 152

piselli all'olio con funghetti *(peas with oil & button mushrooms)*
Cook the peas as above, replacing the pancetta with same quantity of small
button mushrooms, sautéed with the onions and oil until softened.

fave con la pancetta *(fava beans with pancetta)*
Prepare basic recipe, replacing the peas with fresh or frozen tender broad
(fava) beans. Bear in mind that they may need to be individually peeled
before use if they are large and a bit tough.

piselli e patate con lattuga *(peas with potato & lettuce)*
Prepare basic recipe, adding 6 small cubed parboiled potatoes and 3 lettuce
hearts, shredded coarsely, to cook with the peas.

piselli e fave con prosciutto di Parma *(peas & broad beans)*
Prepare basic recipe, replacing the pancetta with chopped Parma ham.

piselli e melanzane *(peas & eggplant)*
Prepare basic recipe, omitting the pancetta. Cut 2 eggplants into cubes
slightly larger than the peas, sprinkle with salt, and let drain for about an
hour. Rinse and dry, then fry with the onions in olive oil. When the eggplant
is soft, add peas and proceed with the recipe.

variations

terrina di peperoni e mozzarella
french bean, pepper & mozzarella terrine

see base recipe page 155

terrina di patate e pomodori con mozzarella *(potato, tomato & mozzarella terrine)*
Prepare basic recipe, replacing the peppers and beans with thin slices of parboiled potatoes and tomatoes.

terrina mediterranea *(mediterranean terrine)*
Prepare basic recipe, replacing the bottom and top layers of leeks with soft grilled eggplant slices and adding a sprinkling of dried oregano to each layer.

terrina di zucchini *(mozzarella zucchini terrine)*
Prepare basic recipe, replacing the bottom and top layers of leeks with parboiled large zucchini, sliced into thin strips.

terrina di patate e funghi *(mozzarella terrine with potato & mushrooms)*
Prepare basic recipe, replacing the peppers and beans with parboiled sliced potatoes and cooked, sliced large mushrooms.

terrina di riso integrale e cavolfiore *(mozzarella terrine with brown rice & cauliflower)*
Prepare basic recipe, replacing the peppers and beans with cooked cauliflower florets and cooked brown rice.

variations

rambasici

stuffed cabbage leaves

see base recipe page 156

rambasici senza la mollica fritta *(simple stuffed cabbage leaves)*
Omit the fried bread crumbs. Lightly coat the finished dish with a little tomato sauce instead.

rambasici con noci e formaggio *(stuffed cabbage leaves with walnuts & cheese)*
Replace filling with a mixture of mascarpone, blue cheese, chopped walnuts, soft white bread crumbs, salt, and pepper.

rambasici col riso *(stuffed cabbage leaves with rice)*
Replace filling with a mixture of cooked rice, toasted pine nuts, chopped garlic, chopped fried onion, chopped cooked carrots and celery, freshly chopped mint and parsley, a little olive oil, salt, and pepper.

rambasici col pollo *(stuffed cabbage leaves with chicken)*
Replace filling with a mixture of cooked chicken, the grated zest of 1 lemon, 2 beaten eggs, salt, pepper, soft white bread crumbs, and 2 tablespoons freshly grated Parmesan.

rambasici col maiale e l'uvetta *(stuffed cabbage leaves with pork & raisins)*
Replace filling with a mixture of ground pork mixed with a handful of raisins (soaked in warm water and drained), some grated onion, bread crumbs, salt, pepper, pinch of dried mixed herbs, and 1 beaten egg.

torta pasqualina
easter pie

see base recipe page 159

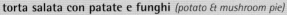

torta salata con patate e funghi *(potato & mushroom pie)*
Prepare basic recipe, but instead of the basic filling, fill the pastry-lined pan
with cooked potatoes and mushrooms, flavored with a little chopped garlic
and fresh parsley. Sprinkle with a layer of freshly grated Parmesan and some
grated Gruyère cheese before finally adding the pastry top and eggs and
baking as normal.

torta salata di spinaci e ricotta *(spinach & ricotta pie)*
Prepare basic recipe, but instead of basic filling, fill the pastry-lined pan with
chopped cooked spinach mixed with ricotta, bound with a beaten egg, and
flavored with freshly grated nutmeg, Parmesan, and salt and pepper. Cover
with the pastry top and eggs and bake as normal.

variations

mosaico di verdura
vegetable mosaic

see base recipe page 160

mosaico di asparagi e piselli *(vegetable mosaic with peas)*
Prepare basic recipe, replacing the beans with the same amount of peas.

mosaico di cavolfiore e carote *(vegetable mosaic with cauliflower & carrots)*
Prepare basic recipe, replacing the potatoes with cauliflower florets and
omitting the asparagus.

mosaico con zucchine gialle *(vegetable mosaic with summer squash)*
Prepare basic recipe, replacing the asparagus with sliced yellow
summer squash.

mosaico con fagiolini e peperoni rossi *(vegetable mosaic with peppers)*
Prepare basic recipe, omitting the carrots and replacing the asparagus with
4 roasted, peeled, and sliced red peppers.

mosaico con porri e carote *(vegetable mosaic with leek & carrots)*
Prepare basic recipe, omitting the asparagus, replacing the onion with
2 leeks, and doubling the quantity of carrots.

variations

torta di zucchini
zucchini cake

see base recipe page 163

tortino di patate e zucchine *(zucchini cake with potato)*
Prepare basic recipe, halving the quantity of zucchini and adding the same quantity
of boiled, cubed potatoes.

tortino di finocchio *(fennel cake)*
Prepare basic recipe, replacing the zucchini with 8 fennel bulbs, boiled and
chopped coarsely.

tortino di cavolfiore e pecorino *(cauliflower & pecorino cake)*
Prepare basic recipe, replacing the zucchini with 1 head of cauliflower, boiled and
roughly chopped, and replacing the Parmesan with freshly grated pecorino.

tortino di fagiolini con gorgonzola e mandorle tostate *(green bean, gorgonzola &*
almond cake)
Prepare basic recipe, replacing the zucchini with 6 handfuls topped and tailed green
beans, boiled until tender, drained, and chopped into 1-inch sections. Add some
cubed Gorgonzola and 2 tablespoons toasted sliced almonds to the mixture.

tortino di carote all'arancio *(carrot cake)*
Prepare basic recipe, using 12 medium-sized boiled carrots instead of zucchini and
flavoring the mixture, before baking, with the grated zest of 1 orange.

variations

frittata di zucchini
zucchini omelet

see base recipe page 164

frittata di fiori di zucchini *(zucchini flower frittata)*
Replace zucchini with about 30 zucchini flowers, washed, dried, and roughly chopped. Mix into eggs along with fried onions and proceed with basic recipe.

frittata di piselli *(zucchini omelet with peas)*
Replace zucchini with about 4 cups cooked peas. Mix into the eggs with the fried onions and proceed with basic recipe.

frittata di spinaci *(zucchini omelet with spinach)*
Replace zucchini with 3 handfuls fresh spinach, cooked, drained, squeezed dry, and roughly chopped. Mix into the eggs along with fried onions and proceed with basic recipe.

frittata di cipolle *(omelet with onion)*
Omit zucchini and onions. Fry 5 onions, thinly sliced, in olive oil until soft and golden. Add these to the egg mixture and proceed with basic recipe.

frittata di porri e patate con taleggio *(zucchini omelet with potato & cheese)*
Replace zucchini, onion, and Parmesan with 1 thinly sliced large leek, cooked in a little olive oil; 3 boiled potatoes, thinly sliced; and 1 chunk taleggio, cubed. Add to beaten eggs and proceed with basic recipe.

verdure alla griglia
grilled vegetables

see base recipe page 166

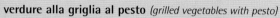

verdure alla griglia al pesto *(grilled vegetables with pesto)*
Omit parsley. Drizzle dish with 3 tablespoons pesto, thinned with extra olive oil, and a handful of Parmesan shavings.

verdure alla griglia con scamorza *(grilled vegetables with smoked cheese)*
Slice 3 scamorza (smoked mozzarella) in half and fry in a very hot pan in a little oil until just melting. Lay on the grilled vegetables and serve.

bruschetta di verdure alla griglia *(grilled vegetable bruschetta)*
Before grilling the vegetables, toast 6 large slices of crusty Italian bread. Rub each slice with a peeled garlic clove and drizzle with olive oil. Arrange in a serving dish, then proceed with basic recipe.

verdure alla griglia con olive, capperi e acciughe *(grilled vegetables with capers & anchovies)*
Chop 2 handfuls pitted green olives and 1 handful rinsed and dried capers with 4 drained, canned anchovy fillets. Gently fry some bread croutons in a little olive oil. Scatter olives, capers, anchovies, and croutons over grilled vegetables. Omit parsley but drizzle with olive oil to serve.

verdure alla griglia con polenta *(grilled vegetables with polenta)*
Prepare basic recipe, adding 12 small slices cooked, set polenta, grilled until crisp and golden. Arrange polenta with vegetables on platter, scatter with Parmesan shavings, and serve at once.

secondi piatti: pesce e frutti di mare

second course: fish & seafood

A visit to Italy cannot be complete without a trip to the local market, where the fish section brims with a wonderful variety of fish, eagerly purchased by the locals. It is always the freshness of the fish that really counts, whatever the recipe.

seppie affogate
stuffed squid

see variations page 195

This very simple and delicious recipe for stuffed squid (calamari) can also be made using cuttlefish or octopus. Traditionally, very small, young, and tender fish are used, but larger fish can be cut to size as required.

1 1/2 lbs. calamari, cleaned and trimmed
4 tbsp. olive oil
1 tbsp. white wine vinegar
sea salt and freshly ground black pepper

juice of 1 lemon
1 tbsp. chopped fresh flat-leaf parsley, to
   garnish

If calamari are no longer than 2 1/2 inches, leave them whole. Otherwise, cut accordingly. Put calamari into a wide skillet with oil and vinegar. Place the pan over medium heat and allow the liquid from the fish to seep out. Then, stirring occasionally, let the liquid evaporate completely. When the calamari are coated in olive oil, season with salt and pepper and stir again. Allow to cook for 5 minutes more, then add lemon juice and remove from heat. Transfer the calamari to a warm dish, sprinkle with parsley, and serve at once.

Serves 6

fritto misto di pesce
fried seafood

see variations page 196

For this recipe for mixed fried fish, you need a well-aired space in which to fry all the ingredients. You'll also need 2 pans to use for deep-frying and to set up a system to keep the fish warm until it is all ready to eat, because you'll be frying it in batches.

5 eggs
8 tbsp. all-purpose flour
1/4 pinch of salt
2 1/2 cups milk
1 1/2–2 lbs. small fish (e.g., whitebait), large
   shrimp, and calamari rings

2 quarts light olive oil or sunflower seed oil
sea salt
12 lemon wedges, to serve

Beat the eggs with a balloon whisk until well blended and smooth. Gradually add flour and salt, beating constantly. Gradually pour in the milk, still beating and stirring. When you have a completely lump-free, smooth batter, set aside until required. Clean and wash the fish and make sure it is as dry as possible. Submerge fish in batter and let stand for about 30 minutes.

Meanwhile, divide oil into 2 deep-fat fryers or deep-skillets. Arrange a large serving dish safely over a pan of simmering water and cover with paper towels to absorb excess grease. In this way you can keep the fish hot as you fry without putting it in the oven, which would cause it to lose its crispness. Heat the oil until a small piece of bread dropped into it sizzles instantly. Lift the fish out of the batter, allow to drain slightly to avoid excess batter burning the oil, and drop into fat. Fry the fish quickly, in batches, using both pans and turning fish over after about 2 minutes. Remove with a slotted spoon as soon as they are golden and crisp and place on the serving platter to drain on the paper towels. Replace paper towels as

soon as they become too greasy. Work quickly, keeping the oil at maximum heat so that fish can cook as fast as possible. Remove paper towels and sprinkle the fish with salt. Serve immediately on a clean warm platter with the lemon wedges.

Serves 6

sarde impanate
breaded sardines

see variations page 197

A wonderfully simple recipe, these deep-fried sardines are often served in piles as party food because they are easily eaten with the fingers.

12 fresh sardines
3 eggs, beaten thoroughly
sea salt and freshly ground black pepper
8 tbsp. dried Italian bread crumbs (Pangrattato recommended)

sunflower seed or grapeseed oil for deep-fat frying
lemon wedges to serve

Gut and bone all the fish, pulling from the head through the fish, making sure the sardines end up whole and flat, but headless, boneless, and with no trace of blood or innards. Wash fish thoroughly and pat dry. Beat the eggs with salt and pepper, then lay all the sardines in egg mixture to soak for about 30 minutes. Remove each fish, let drain by holding it up by the tail, and then coat each one in bread crumbs. Heat the oil until a small piece of bread dropped into it sizzles instantly, then fry crumb-coated sardines for about 5 minutes, or until golden and crisp. Drain thoroughly on plenty of paper towels and arrange on a dish with the lemon wedges to serve.

Serves 6

spada al forno
baked swordfish

see variations page 198

This recipe for baked swordfish can also be used for tuna steaks, or even fillets or steaks of another kind of fish, although the cooking times may need to be slightly adjusted depending upon the type of fish and how thickly the slices are cut.

6 thick swordfish steaks
2 1/4 cups soft white bread crumbs
2 oz. salted capers, rinsed, dried, and finely chopped
5 oz. pecorino, freshly grated

2 oz. pitted green olives, finely chopped
3 tbsp. finely chopped fresh flat-leaf parsley
sea salt and freshly ground black pepper
6 tbsp. extra-virgin olive oil
juice of 1 lemon

Wash and dry the swordfish steaks. Preheat the oven to 350°F.

Using your fingers, mix the bread crumbs with the capers, cheese, olives, parsley, salt, and pepper. Use a little of the olive oil to grease an ovenproof dish that will snugly fit all 6 steaks, then brush the steaks with oil on both sides. Spread half the bread crumb mixture over the bottom of the dish, and lay the swordfish steaks on top. Season the fish with salt and pepper. Cover with the rest of the bread crumb mixture, and then drizzle with the rest of the olive oil. Bake for about 10 minutes, remove the dish from oven, pour lemon juice all over the top, and return to the oven for 10 minutes more.

Serves 6

orata al forno
baked bream

see variations page 199

Although traditionally this dish uses a gilthead or emperor bream, you can bake any kind of large, thick fish, which will cook more or less at the same time as the potatoes. Serve this with some green salad and a dish of slowly oven-roasted tomatoes for a really fantastic meal.

1 large sea bream (about 2 1/4 lbs. cleaned weight), gutted and scaled
2/3 cup extra-virgin olive oil
sea salt and freshly ground black pepper

handful fresh flat-leaf parsley, chopped
4 cloves garlic, finely chopped
1 lb. potatoes, peeled
3 oz. Parmesan, freshly grated

Preheat the oven to 350°F. Wash and dry the fish inside and out. Brush it, inside and out, with half the oil. Season with salt and pepper, and dress inside and out with half the parsley and garlic. Set aside.

Slice the potatoes to a half-inch thickness and leave in a bowl of cold water to soak until required, then drain and rub dry with a cloth. Put the potatoes into an ovenproof dish and add the rest of the oil, parsley, and garlic. Mix well. Season with salt and pepper and arrange potatoes in a thick layer across the dish, then sprinkle with Parmesan. Lay the fish on top of the potatoes, and bake for about 40 minutes, basting occasionally with a little olive oil.

Serves 6

filetti di triglia al parma
filleted red mullet

see variations page 200

This recipe is for filleted red mullet, which is a really meaty fish with a very intense flavor that marries very well with the rest of the ingredients. A good substitute for red mullet, which can prove tricky to find, are small, meaty perch fillets or small red snapper fillets. If you can, buy large mullet that can be filleted easily, as this is a very bony fish.

8 red mullet fillets, washed and dried
8 slices Parma ham
3 tbsp. extra-virgin olive oil
2 cloves garlic, crushed

3 fresh sage leaves, rubbed
1 1/8 cup dry white wine
sea salt and freshly ground black pepper
handful sage leaves to deep-fry for garnish

Wrap the fish fillets in the ham slices. Heat the oil in a wide skillet over medium heat and add the garlic and rubbed sage leaves. When the oil is hot, lay the ham-wrapped fish in the pan and cook gently on each side for about 4 minutes. Turn once. As the fish cooks, baste with wine. After 8 minutes, remove the fish and season with salt and pepper. Add the remaining wine to the pan and increase the heat. Bubble and stir for about 3 minutes, then pour the resulting mixture over the fish. Serve with deep-fried sage leaves. Wash and dry the leaves, then drop them into a pan of hot oil for 30 seconds so that they crinkle up and become crisp.

Serves 6

scampi arrostiti
roasted shrimp

see variations page 201

Fresh shrimp, in all sizes, are one of the most delicious and precious treasures from the sea. They can be enjoyed in a variety of simple ways that really allow the freshness and sweetness of the shrimp to stand out. This roasted shrimp recipe is one favorite.

12 large raw shrimp, cleaned and deveined
6 tbsp. olive oil
2 cloves garlic, finely chopped

3 tbsp. chopped fresh flat-leaf parsley
juice of 1 lemon
sea salt and freshly ground black pepper

Lay the shrimp in a bowl. Mix together the oil, garlic, parsley, lemon juice, salt, and pepper. Pour this mixture over the shrimp and let marinate for about 30 minutes in refrigerator.

Preheat the oven to 400°F. Remove the shrimp from their marinade and lay them in a metal roasting pan. Reserve the marinade. Put the pan in the preheated oven and cook the shrimp for about 10 minutes, basting frequently with marinade, and turning them over from time to time. Serve hot or cold.

Serves 6

pesce lesso
poached fish

see variations page 202

When poaching fish, the important thing to remember is first to prepare the water in which the fish will cook. This is a step that takes virtually no time or effort at all but makes all the difference to the flavor of the finished dish.

1 carrot, scraped and quartered
1 small onion or leek, quartered
1 stalk celery, quartered
5 sprigs fresh flat-leaf parsley
1/2 lemon

sea salt
6 black peppercorns
1 whole white fish or other fish suitable for poaching (e.g., trout, whiting, monkfish, or hake), enough for 6 people

Put all the vegetables and the half lemon in a fish kettle or a large saucepan. Cover generously with cold water. Add 2 pinches of salt and the peppercorns. Bring to a boil slowly, covered, and simmer for about 20 minutes. Meanwhile, clean, gut, and scale the fish. Wash thoroughly under running fresh water, then slip into the water. Simmer slowly for about 10 minutes, then turn off the heat. Leave the fish in the pan, covered with the lid, until the water is tepid. Carefully remove the fish from the water, drain, and arrange on a serving dish. Serve warm or cold with hollandaise sauce, mayonnaise, or olive oil and lemon juice.

Serves 6

pizzaiola di pesce
fish with pizzaiola sauce

see variations page 203

The great Neapolitan classic, the pizzaiola sauce is normally used with thin beef or veal escalopes. The word pizzaiola means the sauce has a flavor reminiscent of a pizza, which in Naples means plenty of fresh-tasting tomato, garlic, and the intense taste of oregano. It works beautifully with fish fillets.

2 cloves garlic, very finely chopped
4 tbsp. olive oil
1 cup chopped canned tomatoes
1/2 tsp. dried oregano

1 tbsp. capers, rinsed, dried, and finely chopped
2 tbsp. black olives, pitted and roughly chopped
sea salt and freshly ground black pepper
12 small cod fillets

Fry the garlic gently in a wide skillet with olive oil for about 5 minutes, then pour in the chopped tomatoes. Stir and simmer for about 10 minutes, then add the oregano, capers, and olives, and season with salt and pepper. Slide in the fish fillets and simmer for about 6 minutes, or until just cooked through. Carefully remove the fish from the pan and arrange on a platter. Cover with the sauce and serve at once.

Serves 6

seppie affogate
stuffed squid

see base recipe page 179

seppie e piselli *(stuffed squid with peas)*
Prepare basic recipe, adding 2 cups thawed frozen or fresh peas to the pan with the
squid as soon as the liquid has evaporated.

seppie e pomodorini *(stuffed squid with cherry tomatoes)*
Prepare basic recipe, adding 2 cups halved cherry tomatoes to the pan just before
adding the lemon juice.

seppie e peperoni *(stuffed squid with red peppers)*
Prepare basic recipe, adding 2 roasted and seeded sliced red peppers to the pan just
before adding the lemon juice.

seppie al peperoncino *(stuffed squid with chile)*
Prepare basic recipe, adding 1 crushed dried red chile pepper to the oil and vinegar
at the start of the recipe.

seppie al vino bianco *(stuffed squid with white wine)*
Prepare basic recipe, replacing the vinegar with white wine.

variations

fritto misto di pesce
fried seafood

see base recipe page 180

fritto misto con verdure *(fried seafood with mixed vegetables)*
Prepare basic recipe, halving the quantity of fish and adding about 3/4 lb.
mixed vegetables such as cauliflower florets, zucchini pieces, and onion
rings. Divide the batter in half and dip vegetables into one bowl and fish
in the other. Fry fish and vegetables in separate pans, but serve together.

fritto misto di gamberi e calamari *(fried calamari & shrimp)*
Prepare basic recipe, using only calamari rings and peeled shrimp.

fritto misto di capesante e calamari *(fried scallops & calamari)*
Instead of basic recipe, coat cleaned and prepared scallops and calamari
rings in seasoned cornstarch and fry in sunflower seed oil until crisp.

fritto misto con la pastella alla birra *(fried seafood with beer)*
Prepare basic recipe, replacing the milk with beer.

fritto misto alla pastella leggera *(fried seafood with light batter)*
Begin the basic recipe by separating the eggs and whipping the egg
whites until stiff. Make a batter with the egg yolks, then fold in beaten
egg whites and proceed as before.

variations

sarde impanate
breaded sardines

see base recipe page 183

filetti di sogliola impanati *(breaded lemon sole)*
Prepare basic recipe, replacing the sardines with small lemon sole fillets.

filetti di trota impanati *(breaded trout)*
Prepare basic recipe, replacing the sardines with small trout fillets.

seppie impanate *(breaded squid)*
Prepare basic recipe, replacing the sardines with small cleaned squid.

spada impanato *(breaded swordfish)*
Prepare basic recipe, replacing the sardines with well-pounded small slices
of swordfish.

gamberi impanati *(breaded shrimp)*
Prepare basic recipe, replacing the sardines with washed, shelled, and deveined
large shrimp.

variations

spada al forno
baked swordfish

see base recipe page 184

spada al burro *(baked swordfish with butter)*
Instead of basic recipe, brush the swordfish with melted butter, season with
salt and pepper, and bake in a preheated 350°F oven for about 20 minutes.
Sprinkle with chopped fresh parsley just before serving.

spiedini di spada *(baked swordfish skewers)*
Prepare basic bread crumb mixture. Cut the swordfish into chunks and
marinate in olive oil for 1 hour. Thread fish chunks onto wooden or metal
kebab sticks. Coat with bread crumb mixture and place under the broiler for
about 15–20 minutes. Brush them with the oil from the marinade as they
cook and occasionally turn them over, making sure you brush them with oil
on all sides. Sprinkle with lemon juice just before serving.

spada con i pomodorini *(baked swordfish with cherry tomatoes)*
Add 3 cups halved cherry tomatoes just before adding the final coating of
bread crumbs and olive oil.

spada all'aglio *(baked swordfish with garlic)*
Add 5 cloves crushed garlic to the bread crumb mixture.

spada al peperoncino *(baked swordfish with chile peppers)*
Replace the capers with 1 fresh red chile pepper, finely chopped.

variations

orata al forno

baked bream

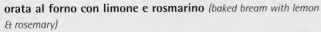

see base recipe page 187

orata al forno con limone e rosmarino *(baked bream with lemon*
& rosemary)
Prepare basic recipe, adding the juice of 1 lemon plus another lemon, thinly
sliced, to the potato base. Replace parsley with chopped fresh rosemary.

orata al forno con maggiorana e capperi *(baked bream with capers*
& marjoram)
Prepare basic recipe, adding a handful of chopped capers and a generous
pinch of fresh marjoram to the potato base.

orata al forno con burro e limone *(baked bream with butter & lemon)*
Prepare basic recipe, replacing the olive oil with melted butter and adding a
little grated lemon zest to the chopped parsley and garlic. Add a squeeze of
lemon to the finished dish both before and after baking.

orata al forno con pomodori e olive *(baked bream with black olives &*
cherry tomatoes)
Prepare basic recipe, adding a handful of pitted black olives and some cherry
tomatoes to the potato base.

orata al forno con cipolle *(baked bream with onions)*
Prepare basic recipe, adding 2 thickly sliced onions to the potato base.

secondi piatti: pesce e frutti di mare   199

variations

filetti di triglia al parma
filleted red mullet

see base recipe page 188

filetti di triglia al vino bianco *(filleted red mullet with white wine)*
Prepare basic recipe, without wrapping the fillets in Parma ham.

triglia vestita al parma *(parma-style whole mullet)*
Prepare basic recipe, using 6 whole scaled and gutted medium-sized red mullet instead of fillets.

triglia ripiena vestita al parma *(stuffed whole mullet)*
Prepare basic recipe using 6 whole medium-sized fish, but before wrapping with Parma ham, stuff each fish with soft bread crumbs mixed with chopped garlic, parsley, and lemon zest, dampened with a little olive oil and seasoned with salt and pepper.

filetti di triglia ripieni al parma *(stuffed mullet fillets)*
Prepare basic recipe as well as bread crumb mixture from above variation. Wrap mullet fillets around small amounts of bread crumb mixture, wrap them securely in Parma ham slices, and hold closed with wooden toothpicks. Then cook as before, adding an extra 5–10 minutes to the cooking time.

filetti di platessa al burro *(filleted plaice)*
Prepare basic recipe, replacing the olive oil with butter and the mullet fillets with much more delicately flavored plaice (flounder) fillets.

variations

scampi arrostiti
roasted shrimp

see base recipe page 191

scampi al burro *(butter-roasted shrimp)*
Blend softened butter with chopped fresh herbs of your choice. Coat the raw
shrimp with herb butter before roasting. If you wish, coat the shrimp with
butter ahead of time and then roast at the last minute.

spiedini di scampi *(shrimp skewers)*
Prepare basic recipe, but thread the shrimp onto wooden or metal kebab
sticks, alternating with chunks of pepper, onions, and cherry tomatoes,
before coating all over with olive oil marinade.

scampi arrostiti con peperoncino *(roasted shrimp with chile pepper)*
Prepare basic recipe, adding 1 chopped dried or fresh chile pepper to
the marinade.

variations

pesce lesso
poached fish

see base recipe page 192

pesce lesso con limone e finocchiello *(poached fish with lemon & fennel)*
Prepare basic recipe, adding 2 additional quartered lemons and a handful
of roughly chopped fennel to the poaching water with the vegetables and
the original lemon.

pesce lesso al vermouth *(poached fish with vermouth)*
Prepare basic recipe, using a mixture of half water and half dry white
vermouth to cover the vegetables in the pan.

pesce lesso al vino bianco *(poached fish with white wine)*
Prepare basic recipe, using a bottle of dry white wine to cover the vegetables
in the pan.

pesce lesso all'aceto *(poached fish with vinegar)*
Prepare basic recipe, adding 4 tablespoons white wine vinegar or cider
vinegar to the poaching water.

pesce lesso al pomodoro crudo *(poached fish with raw tomatoes)*
Prepare basic recipe, then carefully remove the fish from the poaching water
and fillet it. Arrange on a platter and cover with diced fresh tomatoes
dressed with olive oil, dried oregano, salt, and pepper.

variations

pizzaiola di pesce
fish with pizzaiola sauce

see base recipe page 194

pizzaiola di gamberi *(shrimp with pizzaiola sauce)*
Replace the fish with a dozen peeled and deveined raw shrimp. After adding the shrimp to the simmering sauce, remove the pan from the heat, cover, and let stand for about 10 minutes before serving.

pizzaiola di cozze *(mussels with pizzaiola sauce)*
Replace the fish with about 30 steamed and shelled mussels. After adding the mussels to the simmering sauce, remove the pan from the heat, cover, and let stand for about 4 minutes before serving.

pizzaiola di calamari *(squid with pizzaiola sauce)*
Replace fish with thinly sliced fresh calamari to the bubbling sauce. Simmer, stirring occasionally, until tender. Add a little white wine or water if needed.

pizzaiola di tonno *(tuna steak with pizzaiola sauce)*
Replace the fish with 1 tuna steak, brushed with olive oil and grilled until very pink in the center and seared on the outside. Lay the tuna in the hot sauce for just 2 minutes before serving.

pizzaiola di ali di razza *(skate wings with with pizzaiola sauce)*
Replace fish with washed and dried skate wings. Submerge the skate in the bubbling sauce, cook 5 minutes, and remove from heat. Let stand 2–3 minutes before serving.

secondi piatti: carni, pollastri e selvaggina

second course: meat, poultry & game

Here is a selection of deliciously tasty meat, poultry, and game recipes to serve as main courses on their own, or as part of a traditional menu that begins with an antipasto before moving on to the primo and then the secondo.

spezzatino di manzo
italian beef stew

see variations page 229

For the most flavorful beef stew, make sure the meat you start with is of the best possible quality and full of flavor. Be sure to give the meat sufficient time to cook so that it becomes really tender—you should almost be able to cut through it with a spoon. Keep the heat so low that the liquid around the meat barely moves to keep the meat from boiling as it cooks.

3 lbs. (approximately) boned beef shin or another cut good for stewing or braising
5 tbsp. olive oil
2–3 leaves fresh sage
2–3 sprigs fresh rosemary
4 tbsp. tomato paste, diluted in 3/4 cup warm water
1 (14-oz.) can chopped tomatoes, drained

beef stock for basting (page 22), or beef bouillon made with bouillon cubes
1 lb. potatoes, peeled and cubed
1 (10-oz.) package frozen peas, thawed, or 10 oz. fresh peas
4 large carrots, cut into large cubes
sea salt and freshly ground black pepper

Trim the meat and cut into even-sized cubes. Heat the oil in a heavy-based pot with the herbs for a few minutes, then toss in the meat and sear all over. When the meat is well browned, lower the heat and pour in the diluted tomato paste and tomatoes. Pour in enough stock to just cover the meat, cover the pan, and simmer very gently for about 30–45 minutes. Stir occasionally. Add the potatoes, peas, and carrots. Cover and continue to cook for 20–30 minutes more, or until the vegetables are cooked. Taste and adjust the seasoning, then transfer to a platter and serve at once.

Serves 6

scaloppine al marsala
veal escalopes in marsala

see variations page 230

Scaloppina is an integral part of every Italian kitchen. There are many versions — with wine, with herbs with orange or lemon juice and zest, Vin Santo, Marsala, and more. Here is the classic Marsala version from Piedmont.

8 veal escalopes, trimmed
2–3 tbsp. all-purpose flour
5 tbsp. butter

sea salt and freshly ground black pepper
3/4 cup Marsala

Pound the veal carefully until very thin, and toss it lightly in flour. Heat the butter in a large pan and quickly fry the meat, seasoned with salt and pepper, for just 2–3 minutes on each side. Remove the veal from the pan and arrange on a warmed serving plate. Pour the Marsala into the hot pan. Allow the alcohol to burn off, scrape the bottom of the pan thoroughly to amalgamate the butter and meat juices, stir, then reduce the sauce a little before pouring over the meat. Serve at once.

Serves 6

fegato alla veneziana
venetian-style liver

see variations page 231

To make Venetian-style liver, make sure the liver is very lightly and quickly cooked. It must not be allowed to become leathery and tough. Serve with the sweet red onions and a pile of creamy mashed potatoes.

1 1/2 lbs. calf's liver, cut into very thin slices
4 large red onions
4 tbsp. vegetable oil
6 tbsp. butter

1 small handful fresh flat-leaf parsley, finely chopped
4 tbsp. dry white wine
sea salt and freshly ground black pepper

Trim the liver with care, pulling off the transparent, rind-like skin from around each slice and removing any gristle. Peel and slice the onions evenly and very thinly. Rinse them in cold running water, then drain and pat dry. Fry the onions slowly in oil and butter with the parsley over a very low heat for as long as possible, covered, until shiny and soft. Stir frequently to avoid sticking or burning. Then raise the heat, remove the onions from the pan, and keep them to one side. Lay the liver in the pan. Brown quickly on both sides, pouring wine over it as it browns. The liver will cook in about 3 minutes. Season with salt and pepper. Remove the liver from the pan and keep warm. Briefly reheat the onions in the pan juices, then arrange them on a warmed serving platter. Lay the liver on top and serve at once, surrounded with mashed potatoes.

Serves 6

pollo arrosto
roast chicken

see variations page 232

I always serve potatoes, crisply roasted with olive oil and garlic, with this wonderful roast chicken. If you would like to take it on a picnic, cool it thoroughly at room temperature, before chilling, wrapping, and transporting.

6 tbsp. olive oil
3 tbsp. chopped fresh rosemary
4 cloves garlic, finely chopped
1 large (about 3-lb.) chicken, cut up

sea salt and freshly ground black pepper
1 cup (approximately) water, chicken stock
(page 23), or dry white wine

Preheat the oven to 400°F. Pour the olive oil into a roasting pan and add the rosemary and garlic. Add the chicken and turn the pieces over to coat them thoroughly with oil, rosemary, and garlic. Sprinkle generously with salt and pepper, then put in the oven to roast for about 40 minutes. While roasting, turn the pieces over once or twice and baste occasionally with a little water, stock, or wine. When crisp and golden brown, remove from the oven. Serve hot or cold.

Serves 6

petto di pollo ripieno di formaggio
cheese-stuffed chicken breasts

see variations page 233

Sometimes when I serve these cheese-stuffed chicken breasts, I add a simple tomato sauce, either served separately or poured over and around the finished dish.

4 plump skinless and boneless chicken breasts
11 oz. fontina, sliced into strips
4 tbsp. olive oil

4 fresh sage leaves
sea salt and freshly ground black pepper

Trim the chicken breasts and make a long incision down the side of each one to create a pocket. Slip a few strips of cheese inside each breast, then close the incision securely with toothpicks. In a wide skillet, heat the olive oil with sage for about 5 minutes on medium heat, then lay the chicken in hot oil and sear on both sides. When the chicken is golden brown, sprinkle with salt and pepper and reduce the heat to low. Cover and simmer very slowly for about 10–15 minutes or until the chicken is thoroughly cooked and the cheese is starting to ooze out. Transfer to a warmed platter, remove the toothpicks, and serve.

Serves 4

costolette d'agnello alla bolognese
bolognese-style lamb chops

see variations page 234

This delicious way of serving tender lamb cutlets is typical of the rich and succulent cooking style of the region of Emilia-Romagna. Take care when pounding the meat not to tear it off the bone.

12 lamb cutlets
3 tbsp. all-purpose flour
2 eggs, beaten
5 tbsp. dry white bread crumbs

6 tbsp. olive oil (not extra-virgin)
sea salt and freshly ground black pepper
1/4 lb. Parma ham, in very thin slices
1/3 lb. mozzarella, cut into 12 slices

Trim the cutlets carefully, then flatten them as much as possible with a meat mallet. Dip them lightly in flour, then dip them in beaten eggs, and finally in bread crumbs. In a large pan, heat the oil until sizzling, then fry the lamb cutlets on each side until golden brown and crisp. Remove from the pan, drain thoroughly on paper towels, and season to taste. Arrange the cutlets on a baking pan and lay a slice of ham and a slice of mozzarella on each cutlet. Bake for 5 minutes or until the cheese begins to run. Transfer to a serving platter and serve at once.

Serves 6

maiale al latte
milk-braised pork

see variations page 235

When I make this recipe for pork braised in milk, I prefer to use a pork shoulder, which is really very tasty. I serve it with a thin prune and apple sauce, flavored with grated lemon and orange zest. Find a heavy ovenproof dish that will fit the meat and is deep enough to keep it mostly submerged in the milk.

4 lbs. pork loin or shoulder, all skin and
   fat removed
1/3 cup olive oil
4 large cloves garlic, thinly sliced
handful of fresh sage leaves

sea salt and freshly ground black pepper
4 1/2 cups whole milk
thinly peeled zest of 2 lemons
juice of 1 lemon

Preheat the oven to 400°F. Wipe and trim the pork as necessary. On the stove heat the oil in an ovenproof dish until sizzling. Brown the pork all over, then remove the meat and drain off excess fat. Add the garlic and sage to the dish, then return the browned meat to the dish, bone side down. Season with salt and pepper and cover with milk. Return the dish to the heat and bring to a boil, then remove from the heat and add the lemon zest and juice. Allow the milk to curdle slightly, then place the dish in the oven to roast, covered, for 20 minutes. Reduce the heat to 300°F and continue to cook, covered, for another 90 minutes, adding more milk as necessary and basting and turning the meat. Remove from the oven, rest the meat for 5 minutes, then carve and serve with milky juices from dish.

Serves 6

quaglie in tegame
braised quail

see variations page 236

Braising quail is a very easy way to cook these tender little birds because they cook quickly and end up moist and succulent. Traditionally, the birds would be served whole on a thick slice of grilled polenta or toasted bread rubbed with a clove of garlic.

8 tbsp. olive oil
juice of 1 large lemon
4 tbsp. chopped fresh flat-leaf parsley
6 tbsp. Marsala

2 cloves garlic, minced
sea salt and freshly ground black pepper
12 meaty quail, cleaned and washed
12 slices pancetta

Preheat the oven to 400°F. Make a marinade by mixing the oil, lemon juice, parsley, Marsala, garlic, salt, and pepper. Add the quail, rub all over with marinade, and let them stand for about 30 minutes. Remove the quail from the marinade and wrap each one in a slice of pancetta. Arrange them in an ovenproof casserole. Dilute the remaining marinade with a glass of water and pour it all over the birds. Cover the casserole and roast in the oven for about 20 minutes. Test for doneness by piercing with a skewer or fork to make sure the meat is tender and its juices run clear.

Serve the quail piping hot with slices of grilled polenta or thick slices of toasted crusty bread rubbed with a clove of garlic and their marinade juices poured all over.

Serves 6

fagiano al vino rosso
pheasant in red wine

see variations page 237

This method of slowly braising pheasant with lots of red wine works especially well with an older bird that would be too dry if roasted. Finished off with the cream and the truffle, this is a truly luxurious and sumptuous dish.

2 oven-ready pheasant (about 5 lbs.)
12 tbsp. olive oil
sea salt and freshly ground black pepper
1/2 lb. finely sliced pancetta
1 onion, sliced
1 carrot, sliced

1 large stalk celery, sliced
1 bottle red wine
1 1/4 cups light cream
white truffle, freshly shaved, or 1 heaping tbsp.
    truffle butter (optional)

Rub the pheasant all over, inside and out, with a little olive oil, then season all over with salt and pepper. Wrap carefully in pancetta. Put the remaining oil in a large saucepan and add the onion, carrot, and celery. Cook until the vegetables are soft and cooked through. Lay the pheasant on top and brown them all over quickly. When the pheasant are browned, pour wine over them, boil off the alcohol for about 2 minutes, and lower the heat. Let simmer slowly, uncovered, for about 1 hour. Remove the pheasant from the sauce and joint them carefully. Discard the carcasses. Wrap the pieces in foil to keep moist and put aside to keep warm. Meanwhile, push the sauce in the saucepan through a food mill. Return to the saucepan and bring to a boil, then remove from the heat and stir in the cream. Shave in as much truffle as you can afford or stir in the truffle butter (if using), and let the sauce stand for a moment. Quickly arrange the cut-up pheasant on a warm serving platter, then cover completely with the sauce. Serve at once with slices of polenta or mashed potatoes.

Serves 6

coniglio con le olive
rabbit with olives

see variations page 238

This traditional Tuscan recipe for rabbit with olives is one of those dishes that was always served at home when I was growing up. The olives should be small and tasty to give the dish its authentic flavor. Traditionally this is served with triangles of golden fried polenta and braised peas.

4 lbs. rabbit pieces
1 onion, sliced
sea salt
5 tbsp. olive oil
3 cloves garlic, chopped
2 tbsp. fresh rosemary leaves, chopped

3 tbsp. cognac
1/2 lb. pitted small black olives
1 lb. fresh ripe tomatoes, peeled, seeded, and coarsely chopped, or 1 (14-oz.) can chopped tomatoes
1 cup chicken stock (page 23)

Wash and dry the rabbit and place in a large saucepan with onion. Cover thoroughly with salt and place over medium-high heat, moving the rabbit around in the pan to prevent from burning. Allow the rabbit to exude all its liquid, then remove from the heat. This step removes the slightly cloying sweet flavor that rabbit sometimes has. Pour off the liquid and rinse the rabbit carefully. Discard onion.

In a large pan, fry the garlic and rosemary together in olive oil, then add the rabbit and brown all over thoroughly. Add the cognac and flame briefly for a couple of minutes. Add olives and tomatoes. Stir well and cover. Stirring occasionally, simmer for about 45 minutes, or until rabbit is tender. Add chicken stock if the rabbit appears to be drying out. Serve hot.

Serves 6

lepre in salmí
hare stew

see variations page 239

This is a very old-fashioned game stew. The term *in salmí* almost always refers to this dish containing game of some sort. For a dish to be *in salmí* it is essential that the liver of the animal is used in the stew.

2 1/3 lbs. skinned and gutted hare, cut into chunks, and including the liver
1 bottle dry red wine
2 large onions, sliced
1 carrot, cut into chunks
4 stalks celery, cut into chunks
4–5 bay leaves

10 juniper berries, lightly crushed
1 tsp. grated nutmeg
6 tbsp. butter
2 thick slices pancetta, coarsely chopped
sea salt
1 (14-oz.) can plum tomatoes, drained
1 tbsp. all-purpose flour

Wash the hare carefully in cold water. Set the liver aside. Make a marinade by combining wine, 1 onion, carrot, celery, bay leaves, juniper berries, and nutmeg. Marinate the hare overnight. Remove and drain the hare and reserve the marinade. Melt half the butter in a deep, wide heavy-based pot, then fry the remaining onion with the pancetta until soft. Add the hare and brown it all over in the butter, onion, and pancetta. Season with salt. Strain the reserved marinade, then pour into the pot with the hare. Add the tomatoes. Cover and let simmer for about 1 hour, or until the meat is tender. In a separate pan, sear the hare liver in a little butter until browned, then mince finely with a heavy knife. In another pan, melt the remaining butter and mix in the flour, stirring until thickened. Add 2/3 cup water and stir until smooth, and then stir in the minced liver. Season with salt, add to the hare stew, and mix well. Cover and let simmer very slowly for 2–3 hours, adding more red wine if the stew appears to be drying out too much.

Serves 6

involtini

involtini

see variations page 240

Making stuffed beef olives is an excellent way to use the tastier, cheap cuts of beef, turning them into a delicious dish that is perfect with boiled rice or mashed potatoes.

about 2 1/2 lbs. beef skirt steak, cut into
    12 slices (about 3 oz. each)
5 oz. Parma ham, coarsely chopped
2 cloves garlic, chopped
3 carrots, cut into 12 batons
3 stalks celery, cut into 12 batons

3 tbsp. olive oil
1 large onion, finely chopped
1 lb. ripe fresh tomatoes, peeled, seeded, and
    coarsely chopped, or 1 (14-oz.) can chopped
    tomatoes, drained
sea salt and freshly ground black pepper

Trim the meat neatly, putting any scraps to one side to use in another recipe. Pound the meat to make sure each piece is tenderized and of even thickness. Lay out the slices of meat and place a little ham, a little garlic, and a baton each of carrot and celery in the center of each one. Roll up the meat around the filling and secure with wooden toothpicks.

Heat the oil in a wide pan with the onion for a few minutes or until the onion is soft, then add the tomatoes. Season and cover. Simmer for about 5 minutes, and then slide in the involtini. Cover the pan and cook for 40–50 minutes, turning the involtini over frequently. Arrange cooked involtini on a bed of mashed potatoes, rice, or polenta. Remove the toothpicks, drizzle with the remaining sauce, and serve.

Serves 6

il polpettone
classic italian meatloaf

see variations page 241

This is a classic Italian meatloaf, stewed in tomato sauce and usually served warm. Especially popular in Naples, it uses the same kind of mixture as used for *polpette*.

1 1/2 lbs. ground veal
5 tbsp. soft, fine white bread crumbs
1/4 lb. Parmesan, freshly grated
2 extra-large eggs, beaten
6 tbsp. chopped fresh flat-leaf parsley
1 large onion, sliced
1/2 tsp. grated lemon zest

1/4 tsp. grated nutmeg
1/4 cup cold water
sea salt and freshly ground black pepper
1/2 cup fine dry white bread crumbs
1 large onion, thinly sliced
6 tbsp. olive oil
1 lb. canned chopped tomatoes, drained

Mix the ground veal with the soft white bread crumbs, Parmesan, eggs, parsley, chopped onion, lemon zest, nutmeg, and water. Season with salt and pepper and shape into a loaf. Roll the loaf in the fine dry bread crumbs. Fry half the sliced onion gently in olive oil, then lay the loaf on top. Turn it over to brown thoroughly on both sides. Then add the remaining sliced onion and fry for 5 more minutes. Add the tomatoes. Cover and cook slowly for 1 hour, turning frequently. Serve, cut into thick slices, with the sauce, or use the sauce separately to dress pasta.

Serves 6

variations

spezzatino di manzo
italian beef stew

see base recipe page 205

spezzatino di maiale *(italian pork stew)*
Prepare basic recipe, replacing the beef with cubed boneless pork and adding a little grated lemon zest with the herbs.

spezzatino di pollo *(italian chicken stew)*
Prepare basic recipe, replacing the beef with a cut-up chicken, and adding 3/4 cup white wine after it has been browned.

spezzatino di agnello *(italian lamb stew)*
Prepare basic recipe, replacing the beef with boneless lamb cubes. Finish stew with a sprinkling of fresh chopped mint.

spezzatino di vitello *(italian veal stew)*
Prepare basic recipe, replacing the beef with veal stew cubes.

spezzatino di coniglio *(italian rabbit stew)*
Prepare basic recipe, replacing the beef with a cut-up rabbit and adding a few small turnips with the carrots.

variations

scaloppine al marsala
veal escalopes in marsala

see base recipe page 206

scaloppine al limone e vino bianco *(veal escalopes in lemon & white wine sauce)*
Prepare basic recipe, replacing half the Marsala with white wine, and the other half with the juice of half a lemon.

scaloppine alle erbette *(veal escalopes in lemon, white wine & herb sauce)*
Prepare basic recipe, using white wine and lemon juice as in the variation above, and adding a handful of mixed fresh herbs, finely chopped, to the butter at the end of the recipe.

scaloppine all'arancia *(veal escalopes in orange sauce)*
Prepare basic recipe, replacing the Marsala with the juice of 1 freshly squeezed orange and the grated zest of 1/2 orange.

scaloppine ai capperi *(veal escalopes with capers)*
Prepare basic recipe, replacing the Marsala with white wine and adding a handful of chopped capers to the butter at the end of the recipe.

scaloppine al vermouth *(veal escalopes with vermouth)*
Prepare basic recipe, replacing the Marsala with the same quantity of dry or sweet Vermouth.

variations

fegato alla veneziana
venetian-style liver

see base recipe page 209

fegato con la pancetta *(venetian-style liver with pancetta)*
Prepare basic recipe, adding cubes or strips of fried pancetta on top.

fegato con balsamico e pinoli *(venetian-style liver with balsamic vinegar &
pine nuts)*
Prepare basic recipe, omitting the wine. Fry the liver with caramelized onions to
brown briefly on both sides. Then add parsley, 1 heaped tablespoon pine nuts, and
1 tablespoon balsamic vinegar to finish cooking.

fegato all'aglio *(venetian-style liver with garlic)*
Omit the onions and vegetable oil. Fry the liver in butter with wine and
2 cloves crushed garlic. Sprinkle with parsley just before serving.

fegato alla salvia *(venetian-style liver with sage)*
Omit onions, vegetable oil, and parsley. Add a few leaves of fresh sage to the butter
and cook gently for 3 minutes so the butter is infused with sage scent. Then add
the liver and continue with the basic recipe.

fegato con fichi *(venetian-style liver with figs)*
Omit the onions and vegetable oil. Fry quartered ripe fresh figs in the butter until
caramelized, then add the liver and continue with basic recipe.

variations

pollo arrosto
roast chicken

see base recipe page 210

pollo arrosto al limone *(roast chicken with lemon)*
Prepare basic recipe, adding 2 quartered lemons to the rosemary and garlic in the roasting pan.

pollo arrosto alla maggiorana *(roast chicken with marjoram)*
Prepare basic recipe, replacing the rosemary with dried marjoram.

pollo arrosto alla salvia *(roast chicken with sage)*
Prepare basic recipe, replacing the rosemary with chopped fresh sage leaves.

pollo arrosto con le cipolle *(roast chicken with onions)*
Prepare basic recipe, replacing the garlic with 2 coarsely chopped onions.

pollo arrosto con le salsiccie *(roast chicken with sausages)*
Prepare basic recipe, adding 3 Italian sausages, halved, to the roasting pan with the chicken.

petto di pollo ripieno di formaggio
cheese-stuffed chicken breasts

see base recipe page 213

petto di pollo di gorgonzola *(gorzonzola-stuffed chicken breasts)*
Prepare basic recipe, replacing fontina with Gorgonzola.

petto di pollo di fontina *(fontina-stuffed chicken breasts)*
Prepare basic recipe, replacing the fontina with fresh mozzarella cubes and
the sage with fresh basil leaves.

petto di pollo alla groviera *(gruyère & rosemary-stuffed chicken breasts)*
Prepare basic recipe, replacing the fontina with thinly sliced Gruyère and the
sage with a large sprig of fresh rosemary.

petto di pollo al mascarpone col prosicutto di parma *(chicken breasts
stuffed with mascarpone & wrapped in parma ham)*
Prepare basic recipe, replacing the fontina with mascarpone. Wrap the
chicken breasts in sliced Parma ham before cooking.

petto di pollo al Parmigiano e ricotta *(ricotta & parmesan-stuffed
chicken breasts)*
Prepare basic recipe, replacing the fontina with ricotta mixed with freshly
grated Parmesan.

variations

costolette d'agnello alla bolognese
bolognese-style lamb chops

see base recipe page 214

costolette d'agnello alla griglia *(grilled lamb chops)*
Instead of basic recipe, season the cutlets on both sides with chopped fresh rosemary, garlic, salt, and pepper. Cook for about 4 minutes on each side under a preheated broiler or on a griddle. Finish by laying a slice of mozzarella and a slice of Parma ham on top of the cutlets and cook for 2 minutes more before serving.

costolette d'agnello fritte *(fried lamb chops)*
Prepare basic recipe, omitting the mozzarella and ham and replacing the olive oil with sunflower seed oil. Shallow-fry until crisp, then serve.

costolette d'agnello alla fontina *(fontina lamb chops)*
Prepare basic recipe, replacing the mozzarella with thin slices of fontina.

costolette d'agnello al parma *(lamb chops with parma ham)*
Prepare basic recipe, omitting the mozzarella and using only Parma ham.

costolette d'agnello alla mortadella *(lamb chops with mortadella)*
Prepare basic recipe, omitting the mozzarella and replacing the Parma ham with thin slices of mortadella.

maiale al latte
milk-braised pork

see base recipe page 217

vitello al latte *(milk-braised veal)*
Prepare basic recipe, replacing the pork with a stewing joint of veal.

tacchino al latte *(milk-braised turkey breast)*
Prepare basic recipe, but to make it much leaner, replace the pork with
a whole, rolled turkey breast.

fettine al latte *(milk-braised veal escalopes)*
Instead of the basic recipe, make a much quicker dish by using lightly
floured slices of veal escalopes. Fry quickly in butter with a few chopped
fresh sage leaves, then cover with milk and simmer a few minutes until the
milk thickens and coats the veal.

vitello al latte con ripieno di funghi *(mushroom-stuffed veal cooked in milk)*
Replace the pork with a thick slice of veal breast (which can be rolled and
tied around a filling). Spread cooked mushrooms down the center before
rolling and tying securely with string. Then proceed with basic recipe.

maiale al latte con prosciutto *(milk-braised pork with parma ham)*
Prepare basic recipe, adding 3 thick slices of Parma ham, cut into strips,
to the oil at the start of the recipe.

variations

quaglie in tegame
braised quail

see base recipe page 218

pollo in tegame *(braised chicken)*
Prepare basic recipe, replacing the quail with 3 pounds chicken pieces and increasing cooking time by 20 minutes.

coniglio in tegame *(braised rabbit)*
Prepare basic recipe, replacing the quail with 3 pounds rabbit pieces, soaked overnight in water to tenderize them. Increase the roasting time by about 30 minutes.

vitello in tegame *(braised veal)*
Prepare basic recipe, replacing the quail with 2 1/2 pounds of large veal stew cubes. Increase the cooking time by about an hour.

agnello in tegame *(braised lamb)*
Prepare basic recipe, replacing the quail with 2 1/2 pounds of large chunks of boneless stewing lamb. Double the cooking time.

faraona in tegame *(braised guinea fowl)*
Prepare basic recipe, replacing the quail with jointed guinea fowl (for 6 people you will almost certainly need 2 birds). Increase the cooking time by about 30 minutes.

variations

fagiano al vino rosso
pheasant in red wine

see base recipe page 221

pollo al vino rosso *(chicken in red wine)*
Prepare basic recipe, replacing the pheasant with 2 small or 1 large chicken.

brasato al vino rosso *(braised beef in red wine)*
Prepare basic recipe, replacing the pheasant with a joint of braising beef. Increase
the cooking time by about 2 hours to ensure the meat is tender. More red wine
or beef stock may need to be added during the cooking process.

agnello brasato al vino rosso *(lamb cooked in red wine)*
Prepare basic recipe, replacing the pheasant with a boned and rolled shoulder of
lamb. As lamb tends to be quite fatty, you may need to skim off excess fat during
the cooking process.

maiale brasato al vino rosso *(pork in red wine)*
Prepare basic recipe, replacing the pheasant with a boned and rolled lean loin or
shoulder of pork, with all the skin and fat carefully removed.

faraona brasata al vino rosso *(guinea fowl in red wine)*
Prepare basic recipe, but for a much less gamey flavor replace the pheasant with
2 small guinea fowl.

variations

coniglio con le olive
rabbit with olives

see base recipe page 222

pollo alle olive *(chicken with olives)*
Prepare basic recipe, replacing the rabbit with the same amount of chicken.
You will not need to precook chicken with onion and salt, but you will need
to slightly increase the cooking time by about 10 or 15 minutes to ensure
the chicken is cooked through.

faraona alle olive *(guinea fowl with olives)*
Prepare basic recipe, replacing the rabbit with the same amount of guinea
fowl, which does not need to be precooked with onion and salt.

piccioni alle olive *(wood pigeon with olives)*
Prepare basic recipe, replacing the rabbit with 12 small pigeons. Omit the
precooking with onion.

quaglie alle olive *(quail with olives)*
Prepare basic recipe, replacing the rabbit with 12 quail. Omit the precooking
with onion.

costolette d'agnello alle olive *(lamb with olives)*
Prepare basic recipe, replacing the rabbit with lamb chops. Omit the
precooking. The lamb will give you a fattier finished dish and will need
20 minutes longer to cook.

variations

lepre in salmí
hare stew

see base recipe page 225

coniglio in salmí *(rabbit stew)*
Prepare basic recipe, but for a much milder gamey taste, use rabbit pieces
instead of hare.

daino in salmí *(venison stew)*
Prepare basic recipe, replacing the hare with venison. Make sure you use
stewing venison and only about a quarter of the liver.

cinghiale in salmí *(wild boar stew)*
Replace basic recipe, replacing the hare with wild boar. The very strong,
dense flavor of wild boar works very well in this recipe, although you will
only need to use about a quarter of the whole liver.

variations

involtini
involtini

see base recipe page 226

involtini ai funghi *(involtini with mushrooms)*
Prepare basic recipe, but replace all the filling ingredients, except the Parma ham, with sautéed mushrooms.

involtini al prosciutto e formaggio *(involtini with parma ham & cheese)*
Prepare basic recipe, but replace all the filling ingredients, except the Parma ham, with cubed fontina or Bel Paese cheese.

involtini ai carciofi e cotto *(involtini with cooked ham & artichoke)*
Prepare basic recipe, but replace all the filling ingredients with roughly chopped cooked artichokes and cubed baked or boiled ham and a sprinkling of grated Parmesan.

involtini al groviera e finocchio *(involtini with fennel & gruyère)*
Prepare basic recipe, but replace all the filling ingredients with roughly chopped, cooked fennel mixed with coarsely grated Gruyère cheese.

involtini al radicchio e provolone *(involtini with chopped radicchio)*
Prepare basic recipe, but replace the filling ingredients with braised and roughly chopped radicchio and coarsely grated provolone. Substitute beef stock and red wine for the tomatoes.

variations

il polpettone
classic italian meatloaf

see base recipe page 228

polpettone di manzo *(classic italian meatloaf with beef)*
Prepare basic recipe, replacing the ground veal with lean ground beef and
increasing the cooking time by about 30 minutes.

polpettone di maiale *(classic italian meatloaf with pork)*
Prepare basic recipe, replacing the ground veal with ground pork. Omit grated
nutmeg, which can be replaced with finely chopped fresh sage leaves.

polpettone di tacchino *(classic italian turkey meatloaf)*
Prepare basic recipe, replacing ground veal with ground turkey for a much leaner
dish. Replace the nutmeg, if desired, with a finely chopped fresh chile pepper to
add a little heat.

polpettone con pecorino *(classic italian meatloaf with pecorino)*
Prepare basic recipe, replacing the grated Parmesan with the same quantity of
freshly grated pungent, aged pecorino. Omit nutmeg.

polpettone con mozzarella *(classic italian meatloaf with mozzarella)*
Prepare basic recipe. Put some cubed mozzarella in the center of the mixture and
ensure it is well sealed by the meat, so that it melts inside the meatloaf during
the cooking process.

dolci
desserts

Italy has only a handful of traditional, classic desserts compared to other cuisines, but they are nevertheless delicious and easy to prepare. From tiramisù to panettone with zabaglione, there is something in this chapter of *dolci* to satisfy everybody's sweet tooth.

tiramisù classico al caffè e cioccolato
classic coffee & chocolate tiramisù

see variations page 268

When it comes to desserts, this is the great Italian favorite. It was reputedly created in the city of Treviso in the Veneto region of northeast Italy. The name means "pick me up" or "lift me up," and it is supposed to be the best way to cheer up!

10 oz. mascarpone or very rich cream cheese
    (such as original Philadelphia cream cheese)
4 extra-large eggs, separated
4 tbsp. superfine sugar
2 tsp. espresso coffee
4 oz. bittersweet chocolate, broken into very
    small pieces

8 tbsp. weak coffee
6 tbsp. rum, brandy, Tia Maria, or other liqueur
about 20 ladyfingers
2 tsp. cocoa powder
2 tsp. instant coffee granules

In a large bowl, whisk the mascarpone until soft. Beat the egg yolks until pale, then whisk them into the cheese. Very gradually add the sugar to the bowl, stirring and whisking constantly. Pour in the espresso and mix thoroughly. In a separate bowl, beat the egg whites until very stiff, then fold them into the cheese mixture. Gently mix the chocolate into the mixture. Mix together the weak coffee and liqueur. Dip half the ladyfingers into coffee-liqueur mixture one at a time, then use them to line the bottom of a serving bowl. Pour in half the chocolate–cheese mixture. Dip the remaining ladyfingers in coffee mixture, then lay them on top of the cheese layer. Pour in the remaining chocolate-cheese mixture. Bang the dish down lightly to settle the layers. Mix the cocoa and coffee powders and sift over the dessert. Chill for at least 3 hours, but preferably overnight, before serving.

Serves 6

panna cotta

panna cotta

see variations page 269

This delicious Piedmontese specialty is gaining in popularity and fame all over Italy and beyond. The skill of the dessert lies in getting it to set without being at all rubbery, so just the right amount of gelatin needs to be used. I prefer to use gelatin sheets for this recipe; if you must use powdered gelatin, it may be a bit tricky to get the right consistency at first. Here is the basic plain vanilla panna cotta.

1 3/4 pints light cream	2 tsp. vanilla extract
8 tbsp. confectioners' sugar	4 tbsp. superfine sugar
4 sheets gelatin or equivalent powdered gelatin	2 tsp. cold water

Divide the cream in half into separate saucepans. Bring each half to just under a boil. To one pan, add confectioners' sugar. To the other, add gelatin. Whisk both halves constantly until the sugar and gelatin have completely dissolved and the cream is very hot but not boiling. Pour both halves into one bowl and whisk together. Stir in vanilla extract. Cool completely.

While mixture cools, coat the bottom of 6 ramekins (or a 1 3/4-pint mold, if preferred) with superfine sugar sprinkled with a little water. Melt the sugar over low heat to caramelize, or caramelize the sugar and water in a small pan and then pour it into the ramekins. Make sure the caramel is only just blond, so that it will not color the set panna cotta at all. Let cool.

Pour the panna cotta through a sieve into a large measuring cup and then pour the mixture into the ramekins. Chill to set firmly until required. To serve, dip the ramekins into boiling water for 5 seconds, then turn out onto cold plates.
Serves 6

pere cotte nel vino rosso
pears poached in red wine

see variations page 270

To poach pears in red wine, you need to use pears that are not so soft that they will fall apart while cooking. This is a really easy dessert that continues to be hugely popular throughout Italy.

6 firm pears, peeled, left whole, with stalks on
1/2 cinnamon stick

5 tbsp. superfine sugar
1 bottle good red wine

Place the pears upright in a saucepan, slicing off the bottom of each one to make it stand straight and steady. Add the cinnamon stick and sugar. Pour in the wine and bring to a boil, then reduce the heat to the lowest setting. Cover the pan and simmer very slowly until the pears are soft, turning them frequently as they cook so they become completely soaked and colored by the wine. Transfer to a bowl and cool, turning frequently. The longer you leave the pears in the bowl, the darker they become as they soak up the wine.

To serve, remove the cinnamon stick. Serve the pears on their own or with cream, ice cream, or plain mascarpone.

Serves 6

torta al cioccolato

chocolate cake

see variations page 271

Everybody loves chocolate cake, and this one is light and delicious and perfect with whipped cream or sweetened mascarpone, or, of course, with vanilla ice cream.

1/2 lb. good-quality bittersweet chocolate
10 tbsp. butter, cubed
5 extra-large eggs, separated
1 cup superfine sugar

1 tsp. baking powder
2 tbsp. cocoa powder
1 cup all-purpose flour
confectioners' sugar for dusting

Grease a 9-inch loose-bottomed cake pan and line the bottom with waxed paper. Preheat the oven to 350°F. Chop the chocolate and melt it in a heatproof bowl set over a pan of simmering water. When it has melted, stir in the butter. Meanwhile, beat the egg whites until stiff, then slowly fold in the sugar. In a separate bowl, mix the baking powder with cocoa powder and flour.

Remove the chocolate from the heat, cool until just tepid, and stir in the beaten egg yolks, taking care not to scramble the eggs in the chocolate, which will happen if the chocolate is still too hot. Then gently fold the mixture into beaten egg whites. Finally, sift in the flour and cocoa mixture and fold in carefully with a large metal spoon. Turn the batter into the prepared cake pan and bake for 40 minutes. Let the cake cool in the pan, then ice with plain white or chocolate icing or a combination of the two, or simply dust with icing sugar.

Serves 6

torta di mandorle
almond cake

see variations page 272

This deliciously nutty almond cake with a hint of amaretto liqueur makes for a lovely teatime treat. Make sure the ground almonds are really fresh so that they bring plenty of moisture to the cake.

14 tbsp. (1 3/4 sticks) butter
3 1/3 cups all-purpose flour
2 cups ground almonds
1 tsp. almond extract
1 1/3 cups granulated sugar
grated zest of 1 lemon

3 extra-large eggs, beaten
1/4 cup amaretto liqueur
scant 1 cup warm milk
1 tsp. cream of tartar
1 tsp. baking soda
confectioners' sugar for dusting

Preheat the oven to 325°F. Using some of the butter, grease a 12-inch round cake pan thoroughly, then dust with some of the flour.

Melt the remaining butter and let it cool. Sift the remaining flour into a large mixing bowl. In a small bowl, mix the ground almonds with almond extract. Stir the almonds, sugar, and lemon zest into the flour. Then mix in the eggs, melted butter, and amaretto. Beat the mixture thoroughly. Stir the cream of tartar and baking soda into the warm milk, then pour this mixture into the cake mixture and beat again.

Pour the batter into the prepared pan and bake for about 1 hour or until a toothpick inserted into the center of the cake comes out dry and clean. Serve the cake warm or cold, dusted with confectioners' sugar.

Serves 6

torta di riso
tuscan rice cake

see variations page 273

The rich, eggy, sticky quality of this very traditional Tuscan rice cake makes it delicious and incredibly filling. It is like a homemade version of those little oval rice cakes you can buy at all Tuscan cafés and patisseries, called simply *budino*, which translates as "pudding." This is a very substantial cake, so a little will go a long way. Don't worry about how liquid the mixture seems when you pour the mixture into the pan; the cake will set, but it should remain wet and sticky, although firm enough to slice neatly.

3/4 cup short-grain rice	9 extra-large eggs
4 cups (approximately) milk	1 1/4 cups superfine sugar
butter for greasing	3 tbsp. brandy
2 tbsp. semolina	grated zest of 1 lemon

Put the rice and about two-thirds of the milk into a saucepan. Simmer for 10 minutes, then drain, reserving the milk, which will have absorbed some of the starch from the rice. Butter a 14-inch round cake pan thoroughly, and sprinkle with the semolina. (Do not use a loose-bottomed pan, because the liquid will ooze away.) Turn the pan upside down and shake gently to remove any loose semolina. Preheat the oven to 350°F. Beat the eggs in a large bowl until foaming and very pale yellow. This will take about 20 minutes. Add the sugar gradually, beating constantly, then add the brandy and lemon zest. Stir thoroughly, then add the cooked rice and all the remaining milk, including the milk reserved from cooking rice. Pour the resulting, very wet mixture into the cake pan. Bake for about 50 minutes, or until a skewer inserted in the center comes out clean. The cake should be well set and golden brown. Serve when cooled.

Serves 6 generously

torta di prugne
plum cake

see variations page 274

This very simple plum cake can be made with a variety of different fruits. Serve it warm or cold. It is delicious with a little custard or cream.

3 extra-large eggs
3/4 cup superfine sugar
scant 2 cups all-purpose flour, sifted
3/4 cup milk
grated zest of 1/2 lemon
1 heaping tsp. baking powder, sifted

4 tbsp. (1/2 stick) butter, cut into small pieces,
    plus extra for buttering pan
3 tbsp. stale bread crumbs
2 1/4 lbs. ripe plums, washed, halved,
    and pitted
2 tbsp. granulated sugar or light brown sugar

Preheat the oven to 350°F. Beat the eggs until light and fluffy. Add the sugar gradually, then fold in the flour, milk, lemon zest, and baking powder. The mixture should be quite liquid. Butter a 10-inch round cake pan thoroughly, then dust with bread crumbs. Turn the pan upside down to remove all loose crumbs. Roughly slice the plums. Add half to the cake batter and stir through. Pour the batter into the cake pan and arrange the remaining sliced plums on top. Dot with butter, sprinkle with 2 tablespoons of sugar, and bake in a preheated oven for 55 minutes. Remove from the oven and cool before removing from the pan and serving.

Serves 6

pesche al forno
baked peaches

see variations page 275

This very simple baked peach recipe is delicious with light cream, ice cream, or whipped mascarpone sweetened with a little confectioners' sugar.

6 large organic peaches (use a variety that
    splits in half quite easily)
6 amaretti cookies, finely crumbled
1 tbsp. butter, plus more for dish

1/3 cup granulated sugar
1 1/2 oz. blanched organic almonds, chopped
2/3 cup Marsala

Preheat the oven to 375°F. Wash the peaches and cut them in half. Remove the pits and scoop out about half the flesh. Mash the removed flesh with the crumbled amaretti, a tablespoon of butter, the sugar, and the almonds. Dampen this mixture with a little Marsala, just enough to make a sticky texture. Butter an ovenproof dish. Fill the peaches evenly with crumb mixture and arrange them in a dish. Surround the peaches with the remaining wine. Cover loosely with foil and bake for about 30 minutes, basting occasionally, until the peaches are tender. Remove the foil and raise the oven temperature for a few minutes to make the tops of the peaches slightly crisp, or slide under a broiler for a few minutes. Serve hot or cold.

Serves 6

crostata di marmellata

jam tart

see variations page 276

This is the jam tart that is made as a teatime treat for children of all ages the length and breadth of Italy. The pastry traditionally tends to be rather sweet, but you can reduce the amount of sugar if you prefer.

2 3/4 cups all-purpose flour
3/4 cup superfine sugar
pinch salt
3 extra-large eggs

10 tbsp. (1 1/4 sticks) butter, softened
1 lb. jam of your choice
grated zest of 1 lemon
butter for greasing

Mix the flour with all but 2 tablespoons of the sugar. Add the salt. Pile the flour-sugar mixture onto a work surface and make a hollow in the center with your fist. Break 2 eggs into the hollow and add the butter. Knead together quickly to form a smooth ball. Wrap the pastry in plastic wrap or a clean cloth and let rest in a cool place, but not the refrigerator, for about 20 minutes.

Preheat the oven to 400°F. Divide the dough into two sections, one larger than the other. Roll out the larger piece evenly. Butter and lightly flour a 9-inch tart pan. Line the pan with pastry. Fill with jam, spreading jam over the pastry evenly, then sprinkle with lemon zest. Roll out the second piece of pastry and cut it into strips. Arrange the strips over jam to form a lattice. Beat the remaining egg and brush it over the pastry lattice. Sprinkle with the remaining sugar. Bake in the preheated oven for about 30 minutes, or until the pastry is golden brown and crisp. Cool completely before serving.

Serves 6

budino di ricotta
ricotta pudding

see variations page 277

One of the simplest desserts, this is a wonderful way to enjoy really fresh, good-quality ricotta. It is very soft in texture, which makes it perfect for dunking biscotti.

1 lb. ricotta
scant 1/2 cup confectioners' sugar, sifted
3 extra-large egg yolks
4 tbsp. dark rum

1 tbsp. dessert wine such as Marsala or
    Vinsanto
1 cup whipping cream, whipped until stiff

Mix together the ricotta, confectioners' sugar, and egg yolks until you have a thick creamy texture. Stir in the rum and dessert wine, then fold in the whipped cream. Serve in chilled stemmed glasses, with biscotti for dunking. You can make this in advance and keep chilled until required, or whip it together quickly at the last moment.

Serves 6

semifreddo di lamponi al cioccolato bianco
white chocolate & raspberry semifreddo

see variations page 278

The name of this classic dish means semi-cold, meaning an ice cream that is softer than normal. This is due to the addition of alcohol, which slows down the freezing process. Because you can't make a semifreddo without adding alcohol, this makes it a grown-up dessert. This recipe is for a white chocolate and raspberry semifreddo, but you can use other berries, such as blueberries. To serve, decorate wedges with a few fresh berries, a sweet herb sprig, or a few edible flowers, and a dusting of confectioners' sugar.

1/2 lb. raspberries, fresh or frozen
3–4 tbsp. sweet fruit liqueur such as cherry
    brandy
10 oz. mascarpone
2 extra-large egg yolks

2/3 cup confectioners' sugar, sifted
1 cup heavy cream
4 oz. crushed ready-made meringues
7 oz. white chocolate, melted
2 oz. white chocolate, splintered

Mash the berries with a fork to bruise them; then, if you wish, push them through a sieve to remove seeds. Stir in the liqueur. In a separate bowl, beat the mascarpone, egg yolks, and confectioners' sugar together until smooth and pale. Whip the cream until it holds a soft peak, then fold in the crushed meringues. Gently fold together with the berries. Pour in the melted chocolate and fold it through. Fold in the splintered chocolate. Line an 8-inch springform cake pan with baking parchment or Teflon paper. Pour the mixture into the pan and freeze for about 6 hours. Remove the pan from the freezer about 30 minutes before you wish to serve. Remove the paper and slide the semifreddo onto a board. (If necessary, dip the pan into hot water for a few seconds to loosen the edges a little.) Slice into 6 wedges, decorate as desired, and serve immediately.

Serves 6

zabaglione
zabaglione

see variations page 279

This rich, creamy mixture of egg yolks, sugar, Marsala, and, quite simply, lots of air (thanks to the painstaking whisking process) is one of Italy's classic, elegant desserts.

6 extra-large egg yolks
6 tbsp. Marsala
6 tbsp. superfine sugar

Mix the ingredients together in a large, rounded, heavy bowl. Place the bowl over a pan of very hot but not boiling water and whisk constantly with an electric whisk until foaming, pale yellow, thick, and shiny. This will take up to 10 minutes, or 20 minutes if using a handheld balloon whisk. Pour into stemmed wine glasses and serve with cookies or a thin slice of panettone.

Serves 6

panettone al gelato
ice cream panettone

see variations page 280

Panettone is Italy's answer to fruitcake, a deliciously light yet rich cross between a cake and a sweetened bread, studded with candied fruit and golden raisins. Created in Milan, it is first cousin to the pandoro, which comes from Verona.

1 (1-lb.) panettone
1 lb. best-quality ice cream (vanilla, chocolate
    chip, nougat, chocolate, or hazelnut)

Cut the top off the panettone and scoop out most of the interior, leaving a relatively thick border around the edges and bottom. (You can use the extra panettone to make another dessert.) Allow the ice cream to soften to a spreading consistency. Fill the hollowed-out panettone with ice cream, then replace the top. Freeze until about 15 minutes before you want to eat. Slice into wedges to serve.

Serves 6

il montebianco

montebianco

see variations page 281

I have adapted this recipe from the more complicated and long-winded version that ends up with a mountain of cream, chestnut purée, and chocolate on a large platter. You'll need a potato ricer or mouli food mill to make this version.

1 lb. canned sweetened chestnut purée
4 tbsp. Strega liqueur (optional)
3 cups heavy or whipping cream
2 tbsp. sifted confectioners' sugar
1 tsp. vanilla extract
3 large ready-made meringues, crushed
3 oz. good-quality bittersweet chocolate
    (minimum cocoa solids content 70%), grated

1 tbsp. best-quality unsweetened powdered
    chocolate for dusting
1 1/2 tbsp. sifted confectioners' sugar for
    dusting
6 marrons glacés and 12 candied violets, to
    garnish

Mash the chestnut purée as much as possible to soften it, then mix with Strega if using. Set aside until required. Whip the cream, then sweeten with confectioners' sugar and flavor with vanilla extract. Fill the bottom of 6 stemmed glasses (martini glasses work best) with a little crushed meringue and cover with a layer of whipped cream. Push chestnut purée through a ricer or food mill onto whipped cream, then sprinkle with grated chocolate. Add another layer of purée and cover with whipped cream and chocolate as before. Add another layer of crushed meringues, then cover with a final layer of whipped cream. Allow a final small amount of chestnut purée to fall over the whipped cream, then sift the powdered chocolate and confectioners' sugar, mixed together, on top to dust lightly. Chill until required. Garnish with candied violets and marrons glacés before serving.

Serves 6

variations

tiramisù classico al caffè e cioccolato
classic coffee and chocolate tiramisù

see base recipe page 243

tiramisù al caramello *(tiramisù with caramel)*
Prepare basic recipe, adding caramel between the layers. Melt 3 tablespoons sugar in a small pan with a little water and cook until dark golden brown. Once the caramel is cooled and slightly tacky, pour a small amount in swirls on top of each layer of cheese mixture as you assemble tiramisù.

tiramisù ai frutti di bosco *(tiramisù with fruit & rum)*
Omit chocolate, espresso, and coffee and use white rum to soak the ladyfingers. Chop fresh strawberries and mix them, along with fresh blueberries and raspberries, into the mascarpone mixture, reserving some berries to create a separate layer in the tiramisù.

tiramisù per bambini *(tiramisù with apple juice)*
Prepare berry recipe above, using apple juice to soak the ladyfingers instead of rum.

tiramisù al torrone *(tiramisù with nougat)*
Prepare basic recipe, folding in chopped nougat along with the chocolate.

tiramisù al mango *(mango tiramisù)*
Prepare basic recipe, but for a tropical twist, omit coffee and espresso and mix chopped ripe mango into mascarpone mixture along with chocolate.

panna cotta

panna cotta

see base recipe page 244

panna cotta al caffé *(coffee panna cotta)*

Prepare basic recipe, substituting 3 tablespoons strong espresso coffee for
3 tablespoons cream. Omit the vanilla and caramel. To serve, drizzle 1 teaspoon
cold espresso over each set panna cotta.

panna cotta al limone *(lemon panna cotta)*

Omit the vanilla. Infuse the warm cream with the peel of 1 lemon. Remove it from
the cream once cooled. Omit the caramel. To serve, drizzle with a little sugar syrup
(melt the sugar in a pan with water until clear and syrupy) into which you have
stirred 1 teaspoon finely grated lemon zest.

panna cotta al cioccolato *(chocolate panna cotta)*

Prepare basic recipe, stirring 1 tablespoon powdered chocolate into the hot cream.
Omit the caramel. To serve, surround with a pool of melted bittersweet chocolate.

panna cotta al whiskey *(whiskey panna cotta)*

Replace 2–3 tablespoons of the cream with whiskey. To serve, drizzle with
1 teaspoon whiskey.

panna cotta al brandy *(brandy panna cotta)*

Prepare basic recipe, substituting 2–3 tablespoons brandy for the same amount of
cream. Omit the vanilla and caramel. To serve, drizzle with 1 teaspoon brandy.

variations

pere cotte nel vino rosso
pears poached in red wine

see base recipe page 247

pere cotte nel vino rosso sciroppate *(poached pears with red wine syrup)*
Prepare basic recipe. After simmering, drain the pears, reduce the poaching liquid to a syrup, and drizzle the syrup over the pears.

pere cotte nel vino bianco *(poached pears with white wine)*
Prepare basic recipe, replacing the red wine with medium-dry white wine.

pesche cotte nel vino bianco *(peaches poached in white wine)*
Prepare basic recipe, replacing the pears with slightly unripe (hard) peaches, carefully peeled. Replace the red wine with white wine.

prugne cotte nel vino rosso *(plums poached in white wine)*
Prepare basic recipe, replacing the pears with large plums, peeled if possible. (To peel them easily, blanch for 2 minutes in boiling hot water, then remove the skins before poaching.)

mele e pere cotte *(poached apples & pears)*
Prepare basic recipe, replacing the 6 whole pears with 3 apples and 3 pears, peeled, cored, and quartered. Poach them gently with the cinnamon stick and sugar. Replace the wine with water. Serve hot or cold.

torta al cioccolato
chocolate cake

see base recipe page 248

torta al cioccolato e caffè *(chocolate–coffee cake)*
Prepare basic recipe, adding 2–3 teaspoons strong espresso coffee to the melted chocolate along with the butter.

torta al cioccolato con le noci *(chocolate cake with walnuts)*
Prepare basic recipe, adding 1 handful coarsely chopped walnuts after mixing in the egg yolks.

torta al cioccolato al latte *(milk chocolate cake)*
Prepare basic recipe, replacing the bittersweet chocolate with best-quality milk chocolate.

torta al cioccolato al gianduja *(gianduja chocolate cake)*
Prepare basic recipe, replacing the bittersweet chocolate with best-quality gianduja chocolate.

torta al cioccolato ai pistacchi *(chocolate & pistachio cake)*
Prepare basic recipe, adding 2 handfuls coarsely chopped pistachios after mixing in the egg yolks.

variations

torta di mandorle

almond cake

see base recipe page 251

torta di mandorle al cioccolato *(chocolate almond cake)*
Prepare basic recipe, replacing the lemon zest with 2 tablespoons semisweet chocolate chips.

torta di mandorle con fichi secchi *(almond cake with dried figs)*
Prepare basic recipe, adding a handful of coarsely chopped dried figs when you add eggs, melted butter, and amaretto.

torta di mandorle con le albicocche secche *(almond cake with dried apricots)*
Prepare basic recipe, adding a handful of coarsely chopped dried apricots when you add the eggs, melted butter, and amaretto.

torta di mandorle e prugne secche *(almond cake with prunes)*
Prepare basic recipe, adding a handful of coarsely chopped pitted prunes when you add the eggs, melted butter, and amaretto.

torta di mandorle e pistacchi *(almond cake with pistachio)*
Prepare basic recipe, replacing half the ground almonds with the same amount of ground pistachios.

torta di riso
tuscan rice cake

see base recipe page 252

torta di riso ai canditi *(tuscan rice cake with candied peel)*
Prepare basic recipe, adding about 4 tablespoons mixed chopped candied
peel to the beaten eggs along with the cooked rice.

torta di riso alle noci *(tuscan rice cake with walnuts)*
Prepare basic recipe, adding about 4 tablespoons coarsely chopped walnuts
to the beaten eggs along with cooked rice. For an extra nutty taste, toast the
walnuts briefly before chopping them.

torta di riso con le mandorle *(tuscan rice cake with almonds)*
Prepare basic recipe, adding about 5 tablespoons chopped blanched almonds
to the beaten eggs along with the cooked rice. You can change the texture
of the cake further by using ground almonds instead of chopped.

torta di riso ai pistacchi *(tuscan rice cake with pistachio)*
Prepare basic recipe, adding about 4 tablespoons coarsely chopped pistachios
to the beaten eggs along with the cooked rice.

torta di riso al marsala *(marsala tuscan rice cake)*
Prepare basic recipe, replacing the brandy with the same amount of sweet or
dry Marsala and replacing the lemon zest with orange zest.

torte di prugne
plum cake

see base recipe page 255

torta di mele *(apple cake)*
Prepare basic recipe, replacing the plums with peeled, cored, and sliced apples.

torta di pesche *(peach cake)*
Prepare basic recipe, replacing the plums with peeled and sliced peaches. It is best to use peaches that are not too juicy.

torta di albicocche *(apricot cake)*
Prepare basic recipe, replacing the plums with sliced ripe apricots.

torta di pesche noci *(nectarine cake)*
Prepare basic recipe, replacing the plums with peeled and cored sliced nectarines. Choose slightly hard, less ripe nectarines.

torta di more *(blackberry cake)*
Prepare basic recipe, replacingthe plums with hulled blackberries.

variations

pesche al forno
baked peaches

see base recipe page 256

pesche al forno con cioccolato *(baked peaches with chocolate)*
Prepare basic recipe. When you remove the foil from the peaches, add a small square of good-quality bittersweet chocolate to each peach. Allow the chocolate to melt over the filling and peach.

pesche noci al forno *(baked nectarines)*
Prepare basic recipe, replacing the peaches with firm pitted nectarines.

prugne al forno *(baked plums)*
Prepare basic recipe, replacing the peaches with large, not too ripe plums. You may need to use 2 plums per person, depending upon their size.

albicocche al forno *(baked apricots)*
Prepare basic recipe, replacing the peaches with large, not too ripe apricots. You may need to use 2 apricots per person, depending upon their size.

pesche al forno con pistacchi *(baked peaches with pistachios)*
Prepare basic recipe, replacing the blanched almonds with chopped pistachios.

crostata di marmellata

jam tart

see base recipe page 257

crostata di marmellata con le mele *(jam tart with apples)*
Prepare basic recipe, arranging 2 peeled and sliced apples over the pastry base before covering with jam.

crostata di marmellata con le prugne *(jam tart with plums)*
Prepare basic recipe, arranging 9 large washed, pitted, and sliced plums over pastry base before covering with jam.

crostata di marmellata con le albicocche *(jam tart with apricots)*
Prepare basic recipe, arranging 9 large washed and sliced fresh apricots over the pastry base before covering with jam.

crostata di marmellata all'arancio *(marmalade tart)*
Prepare basic recipe, replacing the grated lemon zest with the grated zest of 1 orange, and using continental-style orange marmalade instead of jam.

crostata di marmellata di castagne *(jam tart with chestnuts)*
Prepare basic recipe, omitting the grated lemon zest. Use chestnut jam for the filling and sprinkle it with chopped toasted chestnuts before adding the pastry lattice.

budino di ricotta
ricotta pudding

see base recipe page 258

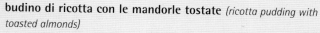

budino di ricotta con le mandorle tostate *(ricotta pudding with toasted almonds)*
Prepare basic recipe, adding 3 tablespoons slivered toasted almonds along with the rum and dessert wine. Sprinkle the top of each serving with a few more almonds.

budino di ricotta con caffé *(ricotta pudding with coffee)*
Prepare basic recipe, replacing the dark rum with the same amount of strong espresso coffee. Garnish each serving with a coffee bean.

budino di ricotta al limoncello *(ricotta pudding with limoncello)*
Prepare basic recipe, adding the grated zest of 1 lemon and replacing the rum and dessert wine with 5 tablespoons limoncello liqueur.

budino di ricotta a strati *(layered ricotta pudding)*
Prepare basic recipe, omitting the rum and dessert wine. Soak small slices of sponge cake in the rum and dessert wine. Then make alternating layers of ricotta–cream mixture and sponge cake in chilled stemmed glasses.

budino di ricotta con amaretti *(ricotta pudding with amaretti)*
Prepare basic recipe, crumbling 6 amaretti cookies into the mixture before folding in the whipped cream. Serve with amaretti cookies for dunking.

variations

semifreddo di lamponi al cioccolato bianco
white chocolate & raspberry semifreddo

see base recipe page 261

semifreddo al cioccolato *(chocolate semifreddo)*
Prepare basic recipe, omitting the raspberries and white chocolate and replacing the fruit liqueur with chocolate liqueur. Add 1 tablespoon powdered chocolate to the mascarpone and egg mixture before adding whipped cream. Before freezing, melt some good-quality bittersweet chocolate and drizzle it into the mixture, stirring gently, to create a marbled effect.

semifreddo all'amaretto *(amaretto semifreddo)*
Prepare basic recipe, replacing the raspberries with about 10 crumbled amaretti cookies and replacing the fruit liqueur with amaretto.

semifreddo al torrone *(nougat semifreddo)*
Omit raspberries and white chocolate. Add about 7 ounces of crushed nougat to the mascarpone and egg mixture before adding the whipped cream. To serve, sprinkle with crushed nougat and melted bittersweet chocolate.

semifreddo d'arancie al miele *(orange & honey semifreddo)*
Prepare basic recipe, omitting raspberries and white chocolate and replacing the fruit liqueur with an orange liqueur such as Cointreau. Beat the mascarpone and egg yolks with 1/2 cup orange blossom honey instead of confectioners' sugar and add the grated zest of 1 orange and juice of 2 oranges. Garnish servings with orange slices and toasted slivered almonds.

variations

zabaglione
zabaglione

see base recipe page 262

zabaglione freddo *(cold zabaglione)*
Prepare basic recipe. To serve the zabaglione cold, whisk 1 sheet of softened gelatin into the warm zabaglione before pouring into glasses and chilling.

zabaglione al vino bianco *(white wine zabaglione)*
Prepare basic recipe, replacing the Marsala with the same amount of medium-dry white wine.

zabaglione al vino rosso *(red wine zabaglione)*
Prepare basic recipe, replacing the Marsala with the same amount of rich red wine. You may want to add an extra spoonful of sugar to the egg yolks at the start of the recipe.

zabaglione alla panna *(zabaglione with cream)*
Prepare basic recipe. Cool the cooked zabaglione slightly, then fold in 6 tablespoons whipped cream before pouring into glasses to serve.

zabaglione al vermouth *(vermouth zabaglione)*
Prepare basic recipe, replacing the Marsala with the same amount of sweet red or white vermouth.

variations

panettone al gelato
ice cream panettone

see base recipe page 265

pandoro ripieno al gelato *(ice cream pandoro)*
Prepare basic recipe, replacing panettone with 1 lb pandoro.

panettone ripieno al cioccolato *(chocolate panettone)*
Prepare basic recipe, replacing ice cream with melted chocolate, poured into
the center of the scooped-out panettone (you will not need a deep hollow
in the panettone in this instance). Or omit scooping out altogether, slice the
panettone, and drizzle each slice generously with warm melted chocolate.

panettone ripieno allo zabaglione *(zabaglione panettone)*
Instead of basic recipe, fill the scooped-out panettone with warm, freshly
prepared zabaglione (recipe page 262) just before serving.

panettone ripieno al gelato col cioccolato pralinato *(ice cream panettone
with praline sauce)*
Prepare basic recipe. Then drizzle each ice-cream-filled slice with warm
melted praline chocolate (such as Toblerone).

panettone ripieno al gelato affogato *(ice cream panettone with brandy)*
Prepare basic recipe. Then drizzle each ice-cream-filled slice with a little
brandy or liqueur of your choice.

il montebianco
montebianco

see base recipe page 266

montebianco al cioccolato bianco *(white chocolate montebianco)*
Prepare basic recipe, replacing the chocolate with grated white chocolate and the powdered chocolate with melted white chocolate.

montebianco al gianduja *(gianduja montebianco)*
Prepare basic recipe, replacing the grated chocolate with grated gianduja chocolate and the powdered chocolate with melted gianduja.

montebianco al brandy *(brandy montebianco)*
Prepare basic recipe, replacing the brandy with Strega liqueur.

index